**in the Christian
community**

John Mallison
(and a small group)

No. 2 in the Abridged Small Group Series

Renewal Publications

207

220.07

(248.3)

Dedication

With love to the Christian Church in N.S.W.

which has nurtured me and given the challenging
opportunities in which I gained the
insights shared in these books.

ISBN O 909202 06 0

Published by Renewal Publications, Box 130, West Ryde, N.S.W., Australia
(C) John Mallison 1978

Reprinted March 1979
Reprinted November 1980
Reprinted March 1983
Reprinted July 1985

Printed in Australia by Bridge Printery Pty. Ltd.,
Sydney.

Foreword

The Christian Good News is essentially a message of hope concerning relationships. The central theme of this series is that our participation in the lives of others gains credibility as individually and collectively we participate in Christ, experiencing and slowly embodying His love, His concern and His power. There are some "games" and workshop programmes included in this book which we hope will act as vehicles through which the Spirit of God can enable people to become more aware of others and achieve new levels of sensitivity.

Fundamental to all being and action in Christian lifestyle is the understanding of, and an adequate faith response to, the Word of God. We believe that the small group offers an ideal situation for this encounter and growth to take place. Some procedures for Bible study are shared which will help heighten interest and facilitate learning and action.

The Church was born at Pentecost in the atmosphere of prayer. The life-giving wind of the Spirit has continued to be breathed into the Body of Christ through prayer. Prayer is intrinsic to individual and collective Christian life but there is certainly no need for it to be a dull routine or experience. Christians today are rediscovering the joy of prayer and the release of divine power. We share some of the contemporary discoveries with you. These are not formulas which will give prayer vitality but may help.

This is the second book in the Abridged Small Group Book Series. These two books replace the four in the original series. We have written these books as a service to the small group movement and because we are deeply committed to the belief that the Church will not become a true worshipping, serving community of love unless small groups are an integral part of its ongoing life.

This book has been made possible by the support of the former Department of Christian Education of the Congregational, Methodist and Presbyterian Churches of New South Wales and since the union of the three Churches, the Board of Education. The kindness and co-operation of many people also helped make these books a reality.

I am particularly indebted to Wendy Cowling who undertook the editorial and production work for the original books,

3

to Janet Wade, Graham Beattie and Douglas Parker for original material and revision work; to Mary-Ruth Marshall of the Joint Board of Christian Education of Australia and New Zealand, for contributions and advice on Values Clarification and on Simulation Games; and to the other members of the small groups who participated in the planning and advised me concerning the format and content of these books: Helen Chapman, Ross Kingham, David Manton, John Paton, Margaret Tarbotton and Tony Winter. The help of Brenda Fowler, Elva Harris and Dianne Sutton and many others is also gratefully acknowledged.

My appreciation to June Bosenquet for her editorial work with this new series.

Without the love, patience and support of my wife June, these books would never have been possible.

We offer this book in love to all those who are dedicated to the renewal of the life and witness of the Christian community.

May Jesus Christ be praised!

John Mallison.

Contents

Kiss a Frog

Have you ever felt like a frog? You know the type of thing I mean—
> stone cold, clammy, ugly, drooping, green, lifeless — all by yourself in the middle of a pond!

I have! And I've met plenty of others. We have one in our house nearly every morning. The only thing missing is the pond!

The frog blues (or should I say greens) come when—
— you want to be bright, especially first thing in the morning, and you can't.
— you want to share, but are selfish.
— you want to feel thankful but feel resentment.
— you want to be honest with others but keep wearing a mask.
— you want to be somebody, but feel a nobody.
— you want to care, but the required effort makes you indifferent.
— you want to make friends, but will they?

If we are honest we have probably all sat on that lily pad in the middle of the pond. Often we have sat there for ages, too frightened or disgusted to jump off and swim. Maybe you're still on that lily pad, floating round and round — all froggy like, fed up and lonely.

Others we meet in our Small Group or in everyday contact come across to us as frogs. They are so hard to love. Their personality doesn't attract others to them. They are either slow, shy, withdrawn and negative or they are dominant, autocratic, forcing their opinions on others. Cold unattractive frog. You feel repulsed by them and want to ignore or throw rocks at them.

A Parable might help —!

Once upon a time there was a frog. He was really a handsome prince under the nasty spell of a wicked witch. Only the kiss of a beautiful maiden could save him. So there he sat — unkissed prince of his lilypond kingdom.

But you guessed it! One day a beautiful maiden saw him, was overcome with pity, grabbed him and kissed him.

Bingo! In a moment of time he stood transformed before her, A Handsome Prince. And you can guess the finish!

So what is the task of the church — to **kiss frogs,** of course.

1 Study in Small Groups

When a group studies the Christian faith and its relevance to life, the Holy Spirit can work renewal in mind and life. Study has always been seen as an integral part of Christian growth and fellowship. Jesus, in calling people to follow Him, said "Take my yoke upon you . . . **learn** from me". He was called a rabbi or teacher.

Jesus called people and taught them the essentials of the Kingdom's way of life. They were to seek the truth and find their freedom in that truth. Jesus made the claim of Himself that He was the way, the **truth,** and the life. To become a follower of Jesus Christ is to commit oneself to a passionate search for truth. The word "disciple" means "learner".

In this call to discipleship, or learning, is implied the importance and possibility of people continuing to learn and grow. It is essential spiritually that we keep alive mentally. Schweitzer said "Renunciation of thinking is a declaration of spiritual bankruptcy". That doesn't mean we have to be intellectuals to be good disciples. Sometimes that can be a hindrance. It does mean that we should not be lazy in our thinking but take every opportunity, no matter how limited our mental capacity, to increase our knowledge of God and His way for humankind.

Paul called the disciples in Rome to "be transformed by the renewal of your mind". There is a direct relationship between the renewing of the mind and the transformation of the life. A disciplined study of the Christian faith and its relevance to the whole of life lies at the heart of vital Christian witness. Many small groups stagnate because their focus has been purely upon emotional response; they have viewed Christian experience as essentially a feeling. High moments of joy, praise and a variety of feelings result from the Holy Spirit's being at work in the individual and the small group. But it is a fatal mistake to avoid serious intellectual pursuit. Indeed it is neglecting a God-given faculty which He obviously would not have given His creatures if it could not be a means through which we can draw closer to Him.

In all our study we need to avoid the other extreme of "head-tripping", becoming too intellectual. A group can suffer as much from people batting ideas back and forth without digesting or assimilating them. It is easy to hide behind a mask in discussion and never let the truth being discussed seep down into one's life. Enlightenment of the mind should be linked with genuine piety. "Be transformed by the renewal of your minds".

Commitment to Christ and His cause is inevitably linked with our study in small groups. In all Christian education enlightenment of the mind should lead people to commitment. A personal response to Christ should have the central place. Commitment involves accepting by faith the free, yet costly, grace God offers to us in Jesus Christ, and a surrendering of our whole being to His Lordship. "Conversion" experiences can be expected to take place in small groups where the Word of God is encountered with open minds.

As the group studies with a genuine desire to discover the relevance of the Gospel for our contemporary world it will become aware of specific claims of Christ in particular situations. Every study should have an element of call to commitment to specific thought, feeling, and action, accepting the risk and the danger which may be involved in the latter.

In the educational situation of the small group there should be more than the enlightenment of the mind. It should incorporate opportunity for an act of commitment, response, allegiance, trust and obedience to Christ and His purposes in our world today.

Helping people to learn and to grow

This is not the place, nor is there the space, to more than briefly open up the complex subject of learning theories. Scientists have attempted to study the process of learning from several points of view. They seem to fall primarily into two frames of reference: those who approach learning as observers of behaviour (the Behaviourists, or those who follow the Stimulus-Response or the modified Pavlovian conditioning theories) and those who approach learning from the learner's point of view (giving emphasis to the holistic, Gestalt, perceptual activity of the mind). The emphasis in this chapter is upon a theory of dynamic learning.

A. T. Dale in *The Christian in the Modern World* says "Christian education is concerned with the way in which we become aware of the total meaning of the human situation in which we find ourselves, what the world in which we live is really like, who we are and what God is like."[1]

The learning which can be expected to take place in small groups should seek to bring change in a few major areas of living:

— our relationship to God as we discover what He has revealed of Himself and His purpose for human-kind in Jesus Christ, inviting a response which involves both faith and commitment.

— our relationship to ourselves as we find out who we are, why we are here and the possibilities which are open to us through divine grace.

— our relationship to other people through new levels of understanding of God's purpose for them and us.

— our relationship to our environment as we gain a new appreciation of this God's creation and ourselves as stewards of His world.

We learn from experience

Learning is not restricted to formal teaching situations. On the contrary, the greater part of learning probably occurs informally, through experience in all kinds of life situations.

"No one factor, no one method, no one endearing human characteristic can be seized as a magic wand which will transform people into life-long learners and adventurers. Nevertheless, one condition becomes increasingly apparent in the learning process, and that is the shift in emphasis from content to experience."[2]

Learning from experience takes place both consciously and unconsciously. A child learns many skills without consciously being aware of the process taking place. However here we are essentially concerned with the development possible when we take time out to think about and analyse our experiences. We could learn more from our rich storehouse of experience. This learning will be made most efficient when we **reflect** consciously and deliberately on what really happened in our present and past experiences. This will need to be climaxed with resolutions for future action based on the insights gained.

In our daily lives we do not generally have time to reflect upon experiences in the structured manner set out below, although learning will be present to some degree. In the structured situation in a small group it will aid learning to study and follow this pattern.

To learn from experience, people need time firstly to look at what happened. They need to **recognise** specific aspects of the experience.

Who was involved and in what ways?

What were the circumstances?

What surrounded it in time?

What were the facts?

The process of recognising the facts of the experience needs to be followed by an **analysis** of it.

Why did it happen that way?

How did the people involved behave?

What was helpful and what was a hindrance?

What was the outcome of the experience?

How did the people involved feel about it?

The learning climaxes with seeking to learn the relevance to other life situations of the learners. This involves **generalising.**

What have I learnt which will help me when next I find myself in a similar situation?

What should I be prepared to do when next I face a similar event?

What specifically would be involved in applying this?

Am I really willing to work at applying these new insights to my own life situation?

Am I prepared to take the risk and make the effort to forsake my old patterns of behaviour and deliberately put new ones into practice?

This kind of learning is called "experimental education". "Its principal thesis is that learning is only learning when it results in some new behaviour".[3] That thesis is consistent with the gospel of Christ. Christianity was never meant to be purely intellectual, it is meant to result in changed lives.

Douglas Hubery in *Teaching the Christian Faith Today* says:

"It is my contention that experience-centred teaching is not just one of the factors in an educational process, but that at the present time it is the major factor."[4]

On Richard Acland's book *We Teach Them Wrong*, he comments:

"What he seeks to do is to relate the faith to a universality and development of experience throughout all time. And the questions he asks of the pupils are always keyed to fundamental experience and need."[5]

Hubery goes on:

"Experience-centred teaching recognises that effective learning does not take place purely through the mind. Nor does it take place purely through the imagination and emotion."

"An experience, therefore, is a happening in life which in varying degrees affects the whole of our being, body, mind, and soul."

"The experimental approach to education seeks to ensure that what is taught is not mere subjective emotion, nor even objective intellectualism; it is both and more than both. It is teaching which affects the whole of one's being."[5]

For an excellent treatment of experimental education in the church, read *Learning Through Encounter* by Robert Arthur Dow. Dow lists eight factors which are basically required to make experimental learning happen in a small group situation.

1. Maximum participation by the learner who is a respected member of the group, not because of his knowledge, but because of the resources of his own experience which he brings to the group.

2. The individuality of each person is respected.

3. It applies the theories of human development, taking into account the expectations of the person at their particular stage of development.

4. It requires an understanding of the small group process — how to interact, the roles people play, decision-making and development of group cohesion.

5. Shared leadership is encouraged. The teacher is an acknowledged learner, too. Other members can then display leadership in areas where they can provide solutions to group problems.

6. Flexibility and spontaneity are keys to learning, wherever they may lead.

7. Experiental learning is personal goal oriented. It depends upon the learner's response.

8. It always deals with living issues. Relevance is its main aim.

When studying in the small group situation, this philosophy in practice could be used in this way.

1.   **Experience**   Begin where the people are by involving them in either recalling a past experience; or providing a present experience. For example, say the topic was "Trust". You may begin by asking the individuals in the group to endeavour to recall a time when they really trusted another person in a most significant way and ask them to share it with the group. In this situation they would be recalling a past experience.

Or, to provide a present experience, you may involve them in a game which requires them to trust another person or the group as a whole, for example, a 'trust walk' or 'body support' games. In these games one participant leads another blindfolded or their swaying body is supported by a circle of people.

There are three forms of experience which can be drawn upon:

a.   **Actual** experiences. These are everyday situations or unusual happenings in the lives of the learners.

b.   **Imagined** experiences. These are outside the immediate experience which can become real experience through the use of the imagination. This broadens the range of experiences which become the basis of learning. It enables the learner to enter into situations, through the imagination, in which he would not normally be involved. Role-plays, simulation games, audio-visuals, films and filmstrips, drama and stories help one to identify, through the imagination, with characters and events which are not normally encountered.

c.   **Devised** experiences.
Experiences of this nature are those planned in which actual persons and situations are confronted which would not usually be part of the learner's experience.
A person may be invited to address the group, a recording of an interview played, a case history studied or field trip planned.

2. **Recognize.** As a whole or in smaller sub-groups the participants then seek to look at what happened, to share their perceptions. They seek to recognize the facts of this experience. (See earlier section giving some questions to use.)

3. **Analyse.** Discussion would follow to help them think through "what", "how", and "why". They would share and analyse their observations, feelings and thoughts — look for meanings, share their understandings. (Again see the earlier section giving some questions to use.)
It is usually at this point that it is the most appropriate time and climate to **feed-in** resources to help in the analysis of the experience. This feed-in of information is an important facet of this inductive method. It can rescue experience centred learning from becoming purely subjective and avoid the sharing of ignorance. The feed-in will vary. It may be a printed resource, an audio-visual, lecturette, Bible passage or recorded resource.

4. **Apply to life situation**
Further discussion will follow to gather the total learning of the previous segments and seek to discover the relevance to other life situations of the learners. Generalising and synthesising will take place in order to promote growth and change in each learner. (Once again, see the earlier section for some questions to help in this discussion.)
The above sequence may vary with all or some of segments 1 to 3 being repeated with different experiences before reaching the final stage. The appropriate time to give the feed-in may occur at another point if the group is sufficiently motivated to receive it.

People learn by doing

"It is sometimes said that people remember 10 per cent of what they hear, 30-50 per cent of what they see, 70 per cent of what they say, and 90 per cent of what they do. While this is an over-simplification and disregards some other important factors involved in remembering or learning (which is not the same thing), it does draw attention to the importance of participation in learning. People learn more by experiencing things for themselves than by being told about them."[6]

14

"The vast majority of people learn through the whole of their personalities, their senses, their relationships. The greater sense of participation and involvement in a situation, the more the whole of one's faculties are exercised in that situation, the deeper becomes embedded into life the lesson being taught in the situation."[7]

The learn-by-doing method teaches the learner **how** to learn. It is generally referred to as **discovery** learning. The learner is put into a situation in which he is encouraged to learn for himself what there is to learn. Involvement and participation are two key words of discovery learning.

Because of the fantastic rate of increase in the amount of knowledge in the world it is becoming more and more important to know how to find knowledge, how to interpret facts, and how to relate ideas and concepts to practical situations. Discovery learning is essentially concerned with one's approach to knowledge.

Learning centres are now being built into schools in which classrooms are open to a central core which is equipped with a variety of resources for the student to use in his learning projects. He is encouraged to seek out knowledge for himself rather than be completely dependent upon a teacher as the giver of all information. In discovery learning, a student's individual needs are more likely to be met.

In many small groups the traditional pattern of the church's teaching ministry has been followed where learners have expected to be told the facts and what to think about them. However, learners are much more likely to adopt an idea they have discovered themselves than one that has been told them. It takes longer to get facts across using discovery learning than it does by lecture, but discovery will be more effective. No one approach is always right and the lecture still has a limited place, but people need to be helped to seek out information for themselves. They must also be given skills in how to interpret their findings and apply them to their everyday lives.

Discovery learning is closely linked with experience-centred learning. It may provide the initial present experience in the first segment or it may be the procedure used to feed in information during the period of analysis.

Let us look at an example of how this procedure for learning could be used in a small group undertaking Bible study.

15

A resource table would be set up with one or two commentaries, a Bible Dictionary, Concordance, various translations of the Bible, a dictionary, Bible atlas and other resource books which bear upon the passage being studied.

The group breaks into sub-groups, the size depending upon the total number in the group, their maturity and experience in using the resources. If this is the first time the group has used these resources, the leader will familiarise them with them and indicate that he shall be available to consult with concerning them during the session.

If a topic is being followed, such as a particular issue or problem raised by the group, a number of different and appropriate scripture passages may be assigned to each sub-group. These are read and discussed by each group and ideas listed. The resource books are then referred to and after further discussion general principles are formulated and written on chart paper. When they re-group the charts are presented with a brief explanation. The various ideas are evaluated. A general statement may be formulated. Discussion may then centre around how the statement would affect their own individual situations if this was then taken seriously. Individuals may then respond by some form of creative expression, write a prayer as a response or group conversational prayer may follow.

The role of the leader

In the learner-centred approaches to learning, the role of the leader/teacher is quite different from that of the traditional didactic up-front teacher-centred approach.

Leader-centred learning is characterised by:

— Emphasis upon facts
— **What** to learn
— Teaching by telling.

In contrast, with **learner-centred** learning there is:

— Emphasis on individual discovery
— **How** to learn
— Learning by doing.

In **leader-centred** learning the role of the leader is that of

Instructor-Initiator:

— Verbal source of information
— Explainer
— Stimulator

— Critic of ideas and skills
— Motivator of all that happens
— Sees groups as a whole rather than as individuals
— Is usually the assigned leader.

This kind of leadership results in **passive** small groups.

In the learner-centred situation the role of the leader is that of **Enabler-Facilitator:**

— Selects suitable learning method
— Involved with individuals
— Leader is a learner-participant
— A guide through the learning experience
— Provider of part of the resources for learning
— Available as a consultant
— Generally elected or "emergent" leader.

This kind of leadership leads to **active** small groups. It should be pointed out, however, that the Instructor/Initiator role and the Enabler/Facilitator role are not mutually opposed or contrasting. A sensitive leader will perform both roles at certain times, the emphasis hopefully, more on the latter.

Know your group members

It is important to have more than a superficial understanding of who our group members really are. It is amazing how little people know about each other in the Christian fellowship. We should know what people are thinking — the kinds of pressures they experience in their homes and their work situations — the books they are reading. We only gain this kind of knowledge as we observe, talk with and take time to listen. This is possibly the main reason why our knowledge of each other is so shallow. There are no short cuts to getting to know people at this level. It takes sensitivity and a genuine interest in people and time.

Knowing our group also involves having some understanding of the general characteristics of an age group. This is particularly important in leading the group in study. Younger teenagers learn in a different way from older teens and adults. Study methods, topics and resources will be different for these age groups. We have discussed elsewhere the fact that people play different roles in groups. A good leader will seek to understand these roles and how to help people who hinder the group. A wise leader will also try to have some grasp of people's emotional or psychological needs and how they can be met through the group experience. This may seem a formidable amount of skills

17

but a good leader will always be seeking to improve his/
her effectiveness. I know many small group leaders who
have equipped themselves more adequately for the role by
studying for a diploma of religious education with the Melbourne College of Divinity. There are also denominational
and non-denominational Bible or Theological Colleges in
most states which offer part-time or correspondence
courses. Check with your denominational department of
Christian Education regarding what is available.

However, let me emphasise that in my opinion the
most important aspect of getting to know group members
is the first point I made — that of taking time to be with
people — to observe, talk with and "lend them your ears".

Recognise their limitations

Many people will come to a group with restricted knowledge of the Christian faith and limited experience. A
leader must be sensitive to this, if people are not going
to be made to feel embarrassed. Some will not know their
way around the Bible, many will not even know in which
order the books occur. So they will have sparse knowledge of its content. Others will have only a superficial
Christian experience and may have never prayed in a
group before. Group members often have reading problems. Others have problems in written expression and
spelling. An alert leader will avoid the deep embarras-
ment which can occur when such people are asked to read
or write in front of the group.

Build self-esteem

"The feeling of self-esteem is important since it is
the point of reference of all one's behaviour. The value
a person places on himself is determined by the extent
to which he feels himself to be an accepted, participating
member of a group."[8]

Many experiences in life help to destroy our self-
image. Christ came to set us free from the shackles a
sinful world has put upon us. He came to develop the real
person God intended us to be. If a leader is to help others
actualize this, then he or she must be one who has come
to grips with who he or she is, has accepted the forgiveness and renewal Christ offers and is daily opening his
or her life to the power and love of the Holy Spirit. A
leader must be able to accept himself or herself, because
God, in Christ, accepts them. A leader must know his or her

limitations and be aware of his or her "gifts", potential, strengths and be seeking humbly but definitely accepting developing and making these available to others.

A leader will then be in a position to help others in a similar search. Self-esteem influences all our behaviour. It is important to accept each individual as a person of worth even when one does not agree with their ideas. "Persons are more important than information". What happens to the individual learner is the important thing.

Help people to change

The Christian gospel is the good news of the possibility of change. Life can begin again. In the Christian small group this complete about-face in thinking, goals and direction can take place through the Holy Spirit working through the leaders and each member. This complete turn around is one form of change, with some it may be a quickening of pace in moving towards our goal through new insights and motivation to see more clearly the way in which we have been going.

Change will fall into different categories — knowing, thinking, feeling (attitude) and doing (behaviour). Another way to see it is in terms of relationships — to God, to others, to ourselves, to our environment. All worthy change is the work of the Holy Spirit. Our techniques, study methods, understanding of people and appropriate leadership may all help but the spiritual growth is God's work. "We plant, another waters, but God gives the increase". A wise Christian small group leader will be sensitively praying and expecting growth in faith and lifestyle in the group.

Preparing the Study

Prepare in advance

Too often teachers and preachers are preparing "late final extra" lessons and sermons! Hasty preparation doesn't produce the best results. (When hurried preparation is forced upon us we can trust God to make up for our lack of adequate time). It is hoped that knowing more about how to prepare an effective study will make you want to spend the time needed to prepare adequately.

The delegation of tasks is not primarily to take the preparation load off the leader but essentially to help others develop their own ministry. A Christian small group is comprised of a number of individuals who are called to minister to each other. And that ministry is not solely in the area of manual or intellectual skills but above all else a spiritual ministry. God has given spiritual gifts to each member of the Body of Christ to enable a mutuality of ministry to each other's spiritual needs.

Involve others

A number of group members can be involved in the preparation of any study. It may be prepared by a number of people but presented by one. More than one member can present different facets of the study.

A vague aim usually results in vague study. You can't accomplish a goal if you don't know what it is. Many groups will follow prepared study materials which have clear aims for each lesson, but will not necessarily adopt the aim as stated. Other groups will prepare their own studies based on the expressed needs of the group. Begin by writing down your specific lesson aim. An aim seeks to state what you want to happen, what you want the group to learn. Be concise and specific. Your aim will fit into one or more of three basic educational goals: Knowledge — thinking, Attitude — feeling, Behaviour — doing.

Have a specific aim

It will help to have an ordered study session. The outline will depend upon the resources and method which are chosen. If you are using prepared study material, a plan will be suggested. However, always be flexible with all prepared material and adapt both the material and the session outline to your particular group, even if sometimes it means modifying or changing your aim.

Follow a plan

In the section of this chapter dealing with experience-centred learning, an outline of an inductive method was given.

Two patterns found helpful are:

1. Establish the life need
2. Discover the relevance of the Christian Gospel to that need
3. Seek a life response in terms of behaviour, attitude and belief. Plan specific action and begin working on it.

and

1.   Study a passage of Scripture.

2.   Discover the life-need dealt with by it.

3.   Seek a response.

Use teaching-aids

Teaching aids help implement learning. They introduce another level of sensory perception into the learning experience. They help hold attention and add interest. They visualise abstract concepts and increase retention of knowledge. When teaching aids are mentioned, most people think of maps, pictures and flannelgraphs used in Sunday Schools. These will certainly be useful for the group but there are many types which should be considered.

Audio aids are numerous. Records of music or talks are available in Christian bookshops. Secular records provide rich resource material. Tape recordings (reel or cassette) are available from a number of Christian libraries or are available for purchase. Creative Resources (Word Incorporated) have a good selection of world Christian leaders. Record your own copy of speeches and discussions from special radio or television programmes or meetings. News broadcasts contain up-to-date material for discussion.

Visual aids which can be used include: pictures, maps, charts, drawings, and posters. One of my sons received as a Christmas present from a friend, a Snoopy wall poster. The poster shows Snoopy embracing Charlie Brown and the caption is: "Dogs accept people for what they are". I can see myself borrowing that poster to use in a small group study session as a discussion starter!

Printed aids, such as books and pamphlets make good resources to draw upon as group studies. Your daily newspaper is a rich source for teaching aids. Certain comic strips like "Peanuts", "Fred Basset", "Dear Abby" and many others have some insightful comments on life. News of people and the world and editorials can be helpful aids to the group.

Projected aids include overhead projector transparencies which are easy to make yourself. Some pre-printed sets are available commercially. A segment of a movie or a single slide can be shown for discussion to illuminate a point. Video tape recorders are available from government sponsored centres and pre-recorded cassettes can be used to feed into them or you can make your own tapes.

What to study

Deciding what to study is a major decision for every study group. This decision ought to be determined by the same guidelines that we use for establishing the group: needs and interests. There ought to be some comprehensive plan or overall design that seeks to give a balance to the study. Interests ought to be balanced by needs of the group.

Obviously, the major study resource for the small group in the church will be the Bible. For this reason, we have dealt with this in a separate chapter. Some other resources to be considered are:

Devotional classics offer an opportunity to get acquainted with some of spiritual giants of the Christian movement as well as a deepening of devotional experience. Works by such writers as Thomas a Kempis, Thomas Kelly, Francis de Sales, St. Augustine, George Fox, William Law, Evelyn Underhill can be obtained in inexpensive volumes.

Contemporary theological thought must not be neglected. Young adults are particularly interested in modern thought. It is imperative for the Church to re-examine its expressions of the fundamental truths.

Secular plays such as Samuel Becket's "Waiting for Godot", Arthur Miller's "Death of a Salesman", Archibald MacLeish's "J.B.", may be studied profitably by having the group read the play and examine the message. Make sure they are prepared for language and thought-forms that may be disturbing.

The contemporary mission of the church is being explored in publications by writers such as Keith Miller, Bruce Larson, Elizabeth O'Connor, Lawrence O. Richards and others listed in the resource section.

Music. Some groups may be interested in a study of the message in folk and protest music. Listening to records and tapes of the music, examining the texts, and pondering the implications of the message may be an exciting discovery of significant new Christian witnesses. The Joint Board of Christian Education publication *Youth Leader* gives practical help in interpreting the media.

Critical issues of the day deserve our attention in group study.

Contemporary novels and the theatre offer commentary on the life of modern man. Your group ought to take account of how the modern writer sees modern man's situation.

Whatever you decide for your study, thoughtful planning ought to go into the decision with the members of the group involved in the decision. If they help decide on the subject they will be more likely to actively participate. When considering resources, it needs to be remembered that most leaders are busy and need handbooks and other resource material that will require the least amount of preparation. If leaders are unaccustomed to leading or expressing themselves about spiritual truths, then resources for leaders are crucial. They need to be aimed at nurturing participation of the whole group. The leader should act only as a guide to the discovery of truth.

While much of the resource material available is helpful, all too often it can be either too lengthy, too intellectual, or not sufficiently related to everyday living. Therefore, all resource material should be carefully scrutinized and if possible a period of experimental use should be allowed with due regard to the spiritual and intellectual development of the participants.

Group leaders at Port Kembla were asked to list what they considered **the basic requirement of a successful study.**

The following are some of the suggestions made:—

— A study needs to answer a human problem and point to a better way of living.

— It needs to be kept simple.

— It needs to clearly set out the aim, especially for the guidance of the leader.

— It must give opportunity for group discussion and provide questions that promote discussion.

— The questions for discussion need to help the group relate the principles outlined in the study with their own needs and circumstances.

— It should be based on the Bible. One comment was, "We do not want another sermon with someone's ideas, we want to know what the Bible says".

— It must have an outlet in the actual everyday life of the group. There is little value in studying about Noah if this is not connected in some way to everyday living.

— A study plan needs to be long enough to give approximately three-quarters of an hour for a study, but not too long so that it has to be skipped through hurriedly, thus missing various important points.

— The study needs to deal with a topic which grips the imagination of the group and holds their interest.

Study in youth cells

Most of the material in this chapter applies to adult or older teenagers. Some of the methods will not be suitable for younger teens.

The youth programmes which are making a significant contribution today are placing the focus upon meaningful study as the basis of all their activities. The effectiveness of service, fellowship, worship and recreation goals is proportionate to a correct understanding of the nature and purpose of Christian faith.

When study is given such an emphasis, the comment of many a casual observer is that young people are not really interested in such serious activity. Experience in experiments in youth cells (and other youth programmes) shows the contrary to be the case. Young people will enter into serious study if it is directly related to the issues confronting them in their daily living. Other factors involved are the use of good educational methods, variety in topics, content and method. The study must be made relevant to the life situations of the young people. They must always be encouraged to interpret belief into behaviour.

Where to start

Before anything is done in the area of study, one of the first considerations should be, "What are the members of the group **interested** in studying?" Too often we find well-meaning leaders informing the group of the study programme they are to undertake. Most young people, especially those in the upper age bracket, don't like to be told what they are to do, and much more co-operation will be gained from the group if they are consulted about the programme of study to be followed. This can be done by submitting to the group, first, an interest indicator (samples of these are included). When the sheets have been completed they are collated and a tentative programme based on the findings submitted at the next meeting for their approval or amendment. In introducing the sheets be sure to clearly explain their purpose and the procedure to be followed in completing them. The subjects listed on the sheet may need some explanation. Where a group has thoughtfully and honestly completed similar sheets an effective programme has resulted.

An alternative method is to break the group up into sub-groups of three or four and have them discuss any of the following and make a list of their findings:—

— "What concerns you most about the Christian faith?"

— "What questions are young people of our group asking?" (about the Christian faith and life in general).

— "What subjects would you like discussed in our group?"

The leader may need to introduce some general topics to stimulate thought — e.g.: "What do you find hard to believe or understand about God?" (See topics on sample Interest Indicator Sheets). The findings of the sub-groups are then listed on a chart. These are numbered and sub-groups discuss them and rank them into the order in which they see their importance. Findings are listed on the chart and a priority for the studies established. In one situation a leader interviewed a cross-section of teenagers not associated with the group using similar questions to those above. He then presented a chart listing his findings to the group for them to discuss, list in order of their preference and make additions.

Leaders should be fore-warned that even with all the above work, young people can lose interest in a programme they have been responsible for planning. Flexibility is necessary in all work with youth. The good leader will keep checking with the young people that the programme is relevant and make any necessary mid-course corrections. It may even be necessary to scrap a syllabus and begin again. For this reason no programme should cover a period of more than three months. With younger groups it should be even less.

Leadership of studies

In younger groups a counsellor will play a major role in leading the study session. However, group members should be involved in the preparation of small segments of the study. With older groups the members should be encouraged to participate more fully in preparing studies. Two or three could form a team to work out the preparation together.

Some instruction and guidance in how to prepare and present studies should be given by the leader. Ideally the leader will work with those responsible outside of the group to help them gather material and develop skills in presentation.

Special resource people may be invited to the group to lead the certain studies, e.g., a science teacher who is a practising Christian may lead a session on the relationship between science and religion.

Sample Study Interest Indicator (1)

Indicate your interest in the following subjects by placing an "X" in the appropriate column next to **each subject.**

	Not at all	A little	Very much
1. God. "Who and where is He?"			
2. "How to live with your parents."			
3. Worship. "Why and how?"			
4. Approach to love.			

Sample Study Interest Indicator (2)

What aspects of or problems in relation to the following would you like discussed in your group?

(a) God ....
(b) The Bible ....
(c) The Church ....
(d) Prayer ....
(e) The way Christians behave ....
(f) How to find purpose in life ....
(g) Human suffering ....
(h) Life after death ....
(i) Relationship to **parents** ....

(The above are incomplete lists of possible study topics. Gather subjects for these by group brain-storming or by working in pairs.)

References

1. A. T. Dale, *The Christian in the Modern World,* quoted by Douglas S. Hubery in *Teaching the Christian Faith Today* (The Joint Board of Graded Lessons of Australia and New Zealand, 1965).
2. Ontario Dept of Education, *Living and Learning* (1968), p.49.
3. Robert A. Dow, *Learning through Encounter* (Judson Press, 1971).
4. *Teaching the Christian Faith Today,* p.52.
5. *ibid.,* pp. 57-58.
6. *Youth Manual* (Christian Life Curriculum, Joint Board of Christian Education of Australia and New Zealand, Melbourne, 1969), p.32.
7. *Teaching the Christian Faith Today.*
8. O. A. Oeser, *Teacher, Pupil and Task* (Tavistock Publications, 1955), p.34.

Other books consulted—

Martha M. Leypoldt, *40 Ways to Teach in Groups* (Judson Press, 1967).

John L. Casteel, *Spiritual Renewal through Small Groups* (Association Press, New York, 1957).

G. Highet, *The Art of Teaching* (Metheun).

2 Study Methods in Small Groups

Groups can come alive by the use of a variety of creative study procedures. The study methods we outline in this chapter will help make group learning more effective, deepen group inter-relationships and create an atmosphere conducive to personal and spiritual growth.

Sara Little* suggests four basic considerations for choosing methods:

1. Methods are to be chosen for their appropriateness to purpose, content, ages, and characteristics of group, and time available.
2. Use of a variety of methods can help a leader to maintain interest in a group.
3. When methods are conceived as a way to help in opening channels of communications between individuals, freeing them to contribute and to benefit from contributions of others, they become something more than "techniques to secure participation"
4. The physical arrangement of the room has much to do with effectiveness of the methods.

Buzz groups

Sometimes talking it out is the best way to settle a point in our minds. Buzz groups allow a small group to work together on a specific problem so that each person has ample opportunity to talk and to think aloud.

The leader needs to allow a set period of time for the discussion and to tell the groups how much time they have, then to move around the room amongst the groups, listening to see if any of them are finding difficulties, and perhaps helping to clarify these, or prodding their thinking with appropriate questions so that they are fully extended in their thinking. After the buzz groups have discussed for the set time the groups are called to attention and the reporters tell the plenary group what their findings are. This is an

*Sara Little, *Learning Together in the Christian Fellowship* (John Knox Press, 1956).

29

opportunity to write down headings to summarise their thinking on the chalkboard or flipchart. Buzz groups often raise issues which lead on to further plenary discussion.

Listening teams

These are effectively used with a talk, or a film or a panel discussion. Choose two or three group members to make notes and comment on the talk, film or panel discussion. They should note areas with which they don't agree, ask for clarification of points they don't understand, and perhaps amplify certain points.

The team may group to formulate their opinion about their assignment after the presentation so that their assessment can be presented by their spokesman; but more often individual members comment on their observations as they choose.

Brainstorming

This is a quick way to get some creative feed in from the group. The group think aloud. Individuals say what they think "off the top of their heads" without any elaboration or any comments from the group. Their ideas are usually recorded on a chart or board. It is important that the flow be maintained through lack of discussion or comment. The group then look over the list and select what they consider to be the most appropriate solution or answer.

Forum of experts

Often you can add authority, interest, and authenticity to your group by bringing in someone who has actually experienced direct learning and who will tell your group about it rather than your teaching the same material from your indirect experience. (For instance, a doctor, a scientist, a missionary or a minister.)

Dialogue discussion

The dialogue discussion is very similar to the panel discussion, the main difference being that there are two people and the discussion is carefully prepared beforehand. An endeavour is made to develop a theme in an orderly, planned sequence. It may be between those who hold contrary opinions. There is no need in this case for a moderator, although a chairman is necessary for the opening and closing. A dialogue discussion can be followed by questions and discussion if desired. A further adaptation of this procedure is to have written questions submitted in advance by the group, who then hear answers in the form of prepared dialogue discussions.

Debate

In this well-known group procedure, two teams of speakers take up opposing positions in regard to a chosen question and make prepared speeches to a definite time schedule and in a definite order. The debate may be followed by an adjudication or by comments from the whole group.

Research and reports

This may be carried out by individuals or small sub-groups. A problem may have been raised by the group or more information needed on a particular issue which requires further study and research outside. It may take many forms, including study of books and periodicals, interviews or opinion polls. Each person or group is assigned different aspects to research and report back to the group.

Lecturette by members

A member can be asked to prepare a paper and read it to the group at a subsequent meeting. This has the advantage of being an excellent discipline for the member who prepares the paper. This person will benefit greatly in his grasp of the subject as he or she is forced to marshal his or her thoughts and present them in an orderly fashion in black and white. In addition, the invitation to prepare a paper gives to a member who has something important to say to the group, an opportunity that is denied him in a general discussion. A member who contributes little to the group could well benefit by being asked to prepare a lecturette.

Observation trips

The group as a whole or in sub-groups, will visit a situation to gain first hand information and then report back to the group. For example, not all the group may be aware of the facts concerning an aspect of social concern in their community. It will help to observe this in order to make a decision regarding action the group should initiate.

Creative writing

The forms here are innumerable; creative writing to explore a personal response, free imaginative writing stimulated by narrative or drama (e.g. a letter from Ruth to Naomi, The Good Samaritan's diary for the day, brief letter from Paul to a modern boy or girl, or a Church in a troubled area), the writing of modern parables (see *God is for Real Man* by Carl Burke), or a modern creation-myth; dialogue between two Biblical or historical characters; narrative of a newspaper report of a Biblical incident (the group can work together to produce a newspaper of the day of the incident as a project), a newspaper report of an incident which might find its way into a 'Twentieth Century Bible', skits of contemporary situations, biographies, or chapters from biographies, of historical, contemporary, or imaginative characters, essays on a stimulating subject, poems stimulated by thinking through an experience, prayers to consolidate learning on a particular topic, new words for hymns.

Role-playing

Role-playing is simply the spontaneous acting out of a situation or incident (without any script) by selected members of a group, followed by a group analysis of the experience. The main purpose of role-playing is to help people to enter realistically (to "feel" into) human problems and real life situations, into the way people feel, and into the difficulties people face in their human relationships.

In preparing individuals for their roles, they should be helped NOT in terms of what to say, but of "feeling in and with" the emotions, attitudes, life outlooks, of the person they are to portray, particularly in relation to the situation concerned. They endeavour to "sympathetically become" another person.

The leader would need to prepare name tags for the various characters, so that these can be pinned on at the beginning of the action. Each participant taking part thus

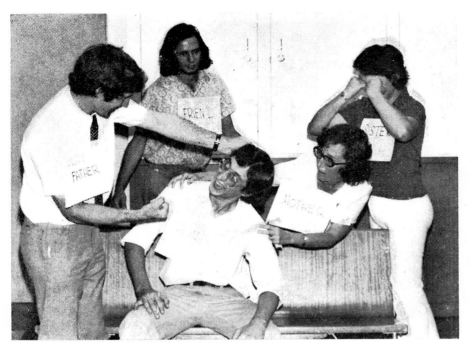

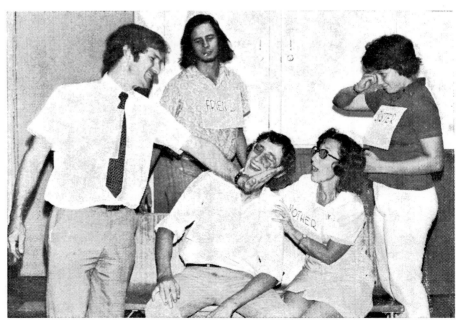

assumes the role of a particular person and loses his own identity. The role play needs to be preceded by a short "setting of the scene" and discussion of the types of feelings and reactions which could be expected in this situation, so that the group members can "feel" their way into the experience.

The role play also needs to be broken off before the problem has been solved as usefulness lies in the discussion which is provoked. A second role play might then be performed which brings the problem to a successful conclusion. After the action of the play is complete, participants need to remove their name tags, thereby "de-roling". Care should be taken when "en-roling" the characters not to cast a person in a role that could be the one that person normally assumes, as this can lead to problems where the person is concerned, especially during the ensuing discussion. Role plays need to be followed up by discussion of the experiences of the play, or of the thoughts or feelings expressed therein, remembering to keep discussion to the roles played, **not** to the person who played the particular role under discussion.

Play reading or skits

Here again, participants could have name tags for the characters, and be en-roled for the duration of the play being read. The character would need to have a complete copy of the scene in which he "appears". The group can set the scene with available equipment in the room, and perform and play out in front of the group. The leader and group members can also have a copy of the play and follow the dialogue in it.

When discussion follows this (and role plays), it should not be of the actual reading or performance, keeping discussion to the characters and action of the play.

It is useful sometimes to call for volunteers for the parts the week before the session and give each character his own copy so that he can read it through at home, thus building up confidence.

Simulation games

Simulation Games are used to enable people get the feelings involved in a situation which would normally be be impossible in real life. They assist the participants to act with a greater sense of purpose and understanding and help to confront conflict and recognise the effects of possible change in a simulated manner.

To grasp what is meant by simulation, it would be helpful to understand the purpose of flight simulators in training aircraft crews and driving simulators to teach drivers of motor vehicles. They provide an imaginary situation which has all of the aspects of the real and help the participants to become thoroughly absorbed in the experience and gain skills and understandings to help handle those situations.

They fall into two basic categories: board games and role plays.

The board games have some similarity to Monopoly or Ludo and the role plays follow the basic structure of a role play but are far more complex in presenting various aspects of human interaction.

A helpful book introducing these games and their use together with outlines of a variety of simulation games are found in the Joint Board of Christian Education Youth Work Guide *Using Simulation Games.*

A second volume, *More Simulation Games*, is available containing over twenty new games, many developed by Australians.

Case study

A discussion on a human situation can be introduced by taking a real life case. Instead of posing a problem in general terms, the problem comes to life in an actual example. Great interest is aroused when a member is able to say to the group "Here is a real life case". The subsequent discussion helps members to deepen their insights into their own needs and problems. In selecting and stating the case, however, great care must be taken to see that members do not become aware of the identity of the persons involved. It is best to take the case from an occurrence in some distant town and even then names and circumstances should be changed to safeguard anonymity.

Case studies are not limited to real life cases. Often it will be best to use an imagined case which is true to life but not that of an actual person.

Values clarification

Most, if not all of us, do not live by the values we profess. We subscribe to ideal values: The Golden Rule, Love Your Neighbour. But are they really our values?

We have two sets of values: our idealized values and our "operational values". Our "operational values" are the partly unconscious needs that really activate us. They are our real values: values which are not reflected in our behaviour are "idealized", seen as a goal, aim or purpose.

Abstract concepts like justice, loyalty and honesty do not always motivate us as much as our own inner need to do something daring, feel important about it and gain recognition and approval. Because the value dimension of our life is very personal, values are often words beginning with "self", such as self-work, self-respect, self-esteem.

In discussing the values our society lives by or that we in the church live by, we ought to begin with ourselves. By what values do I live? Where did I acquire them? Are they worthy? If not, how can I change them? This is what values clarification is all about — clarifying what we do value, and planning how to put our desired values more significantly to work in our lives. It emphasizes a process of valuing, rather than content of specific values or value-systems.

Values are "those standards of desirability by which we choose between alternate models of behaviour". We acquire them through personal relationships, by their being taught and modelled for us. Ages one to five are critical for value formation. Early in life, we set our sails in certain directions. Or they are set for us. Values are "internalized" by the rewards and punishments held out to us by our parents, but even more by identifying with certain people — parents and/or others — as "heroes" whom we wish to follow.

Can we change our values at a later date? Yes, though the process may take some real diligence and discipline. It is not likely to happen suddenly. It requires looking carefully at our choices, actions and pattern of behaviour to determine the values motivating our lives. If change is desired, we can move from there. If we find out, for instance, that we are driven by a great need for the approval of our peers and that this sometimes leads us to act in conflict with other desired values, we need to find out why this conflict exists. We can then work to harmonize our ideal and our operational values.

If we find this hard, and we probably will, it ought first of all, to make us more understanding of others whom we easily criticise, and second, make us search for the resources that can help us in our new resolve. Christians find nothing better than the grace of God incarnate in the Lord Jesus Christ through His death and resurrection. While it is always directly available to us personally and directly nevertheless it comes with special vitality through a microcosm of the Body of Christ — in a small group of Christians who both accept us for what we are and hold us to what we purpose to be.

Values clarification involves a series of strategies that do not force one set of "right values" down everyone's throat. Nor down anyone's throat. Instead, values clarification tends to raise issues, to confront us with inconsistencies, to get us to sort out personal values in a unique way and at an appropriate place. This kind of approach will help you look deeper into yourself and make judgments concerning prized values and to help sort out feelings, attitudes, and behaviour, all those things that are merely value indicators. When we realize the extent to which values guide our lives — consciously or unconsciously — it's understandable that people with few values tend to be apathetic, conforming, inconsistent, and what psychologists often call ambivalent (the simultaneous existence of conflicting emotions, such as love and hate). The less we understand about values, the more confused our lives are. The more we understand about values, the more able we are to make satisfactory choices and take appropriate action.

The person who has clarified his or her values will perform zestful, independent, consistent, and decisive "acts of courage" — not necessarily dramatic, much-publicized feats of heroism, but rather acts based on the courage to say what has to be said and to do what needs to be done.

Using Values Clarification

Values Clarification is not possible unless people can enter into some degree of honesty (feel they trust one another), are open to change, and are willing to explore the values dimension. Certainly the strategies are useful for other purposes (self-understanding, for instance, or developing group relationships), but this should not be considered clarification of values.

They are not meant to be an end in themselves, but are a part of values education as a whole. Having clarified our own values, discovered what we do indeed value, we can then plan action which makes the values more effective in our lives. Or we may plan to move towards new values, towards our "idealized" values. It is at this point, after having clarified our values, that we can look to the Bible and other evidences of God's revelation for guidelines toward a Christian value system. There is not a ready set of values in the Bible. Rather, our values as Christians come to light in the interaction between our particular situation and our knowledge of the absolute value of love as revealed by God in Jesus Christ.

37

Though Values Clarification Games are very good learning experiences there are some guidelines of which you should be aware.

- Do not coerce anyone into participating.
- It should be remembered that values change and perception might even change during the exercise itself. For example, a person could say one thing on a given occasion and weeks or months later express quite different values. A person's answer must be respected as the right one for that person at that time.
- Values are often decided not in the light of what I do value but in the light of what I think the group will expect of me. In other words, my expression of values, or even my values themselves may be influenced by the peer group. The often quoted experiments of S. E. Asch on judgments made subject to group pressure give examples of this kind of change in values. (The experiments referred to can be found described in any good introductory psychology text book and are quite readable.) Leaders might ask such questions as "Can you describe a time when that was true?" or "What makes you say that?"
- It should be remembered that prevailing conditions at or around the time will affect expression of values. The fact that a recent good or bad experience could seriously affect what we say should not be underestimated. For this reason, Values Clarification should never be used as a "one-shot", gimmick approach. A series of exercises will help a person explore their true feelings.
- The leader of any exercise should not prejudice the group's experience by giving specific examples of what happened when he took part or of what he saw happen somewhere else. He introduces, explains the strategy and clarifies any points, and participates as a member of the group.
- Make sure that you have all materials required for the exercise.
- Allow plenty of time for discussion, usually in very small groups.
- In youth groups, encourage younger group members to sit far enough apart to do their own work.
- Values are very personal and should be treated with respect. Build an aura of trust before exploring values. Confidences must not be betrayed.
- Build in frequent opportunities for individuals to reflect on what they are learning about their own values, themselves, and what they would like to do for the future.

See pp. 193 to 197 for examples of games.

3   Bible Study in Small Groups

Many reasons have been given why the Bible should receive serious attention. William Barclay in his book *Introducing the Bible* sets forth a number of convincing reasons He commences by drawing attention to the first chapter of the Westminster Confession of Faith where it states that the books of the Bible 'are given by inspiration of God, to be the rule of faith and life'. It goes on, 'the whole counsel of God, concerning all things necessary for His own glory, man's salvation, faith and life, is either expressly set down in Scripture, or by good and necessary consequence may be deduced from Scripture; unto which nothing at any time is to be added, whether by new revelations of the Spirit, or traditions of men'. That is a tremendous position given to the Bible in the Christian community. It means that 'the Church accepts this ancient book as having final and binding authority.'[1]

Barclay then goes on to explore why the Bible is so special. He begins by suggesting some minor reasons such as it being 'an immortal work of literature', 'an indispensable history book', 'an important linguistic book', and 'a treasury of ethical wisdom'. He claims we get closer to the reason for its uniqueness by reflecting on its effectiveness and he quotes a few examples of lives which have been dramatically transformed by reading it. Barclay says the Bible is still relevant and powerful because it is about people, and about personal relationships. This means it is always relevant because people essentially don't change from one generation to another.

The last and supreme reason he gives why the Bible is unique and for ever indispensable is that "The Bible is the one place where we find Jesus Christ. The Bible is literally the only source book for the life and the words and the teaching of Jesus. Take the Bible away, and we would be left with fugitive memories, and subjective opinions. And this is inextricably linked with the last point we made. It is only in and through Jesus Christ that our relationship with our fellowmen is the relationship of love, and that our relationship with God is possible at all. In it alone we are confronted with the portrait of the one person in heaven in whom these relationships become what they ought to be."

The Bible can fulfil its purpose as it is studied individually or collectively. The individual has every right and certainly the responsibility to study the Bible in solitude, but its origins and the very nature of the church as a community of believers dictates the need for its study in groups as well. Experience through the centuries has shown that the Scriptures release their message and power more fully when considered in groups.

The Bible is a book by and for small groups

"The Bible was written in the midst of a fellowship of devoted persons and for use by such groups. This is true of both the Old and the New Testaments. The stories of Israel's past came into existence at the outset around the campfires of Hebrew desert chieftains or in the company of those who gathered at local shrines to worship. Here they were told to the members of the tribe, family, or pilgrim devotees. And later, when they were brought together, written down, and edited, it was a group of devoted scribes who undertook the task.

"In the case of the prophets, they too were inspired and fired to cry out as they mingled with the people at the sanctuaries or in the marketplace. And the messages they uttered were almost invariably addressed to communities rather than to individual persons. Many of the psalms came into being in the midst of just such a setting, so that when collected they became the hymnbook of the second temple and were used by groups at worship.

"The New Testament may also be said to have been written by a group, the Christian community, and for the Christian community, known as a fellowship in Christ. And this is true even though individuals did the writing. They wrote not outside the Church but as members of the Church. In those cases in which epistles were addressed to specific persons such

40

as Timothy and Titus, the same thing is true. It was the Christian community that was in the author's mind as he penned his messages.

"The Gospels offer a particular dramatic example of the group character of the writing of the Scriptures. We now know quite definitely that these great documents were not the free compositions of individual persons. The authors were compilers, editors, and interpreters of narratives and sayings which had first been preserved by the early Christian communities. And this preservation came about because these materials were needed within the Christian fellowship as it defined its faith and sought to live as a community of its Lord. In a very real sense it may be said that the Gospels were composed as curriculum materials for the first Christian groups. All of this means that when the Bible is approached through group study, it is being faced in harmony with the very best setting within which it came into being."2

The Bible— a book for individuals

While the Bible can come alive when studied in small groups, group members need to be encouraged to encounter God's word individually. The group life will be more vital when each member's spiritual life has been enriched through the discipline of regular and systematic study of the Scripture in private. The very nature of the church as a community of believers dictates the need for group study but this must be balanced by each individual exercising their right and certainly their responsibility to study the Bible in solitude.

While the Bible is a book which comes out of communities for use in communities it will help to keep in mind that so much of it grew out of God's dealings with individuals and their response to Him. As far back as the time of the psalmists, individuals turned to the sacred writings for strength, guidance, and inspiration. This is what the author of Psalm 1 is proclaiming, for to him the Law was equivalent to what we mean by the Bible. Listen to him as he says:

"Blessed is the man who walks not in the council of the wicked,
Nor stands in the way of sinners,
Nor sits in the seat of scoffers;

But his delight is in the law of the Lord,
And on his law he meditates day and night."

This ancient writer had discovered that continuous personal meditation upon the Scriptures kept life stable, fresh, and growing. And there was more to it; a person who did this had a fruitful existence. He counted for something where he lived as, day and night, he meditated upon their contents.

"Every Christian is called (2 Timothy 2:15) to be a literate citizen of our whole Christian tradition. One can hardly hope to be a mature Christian without some understanding of the nature, purpose, and content of the Bible. The Bible is not an elective but a required course for those who seek a deeper understanding of the faith they profess. In any case, if a Christian is to move toward the kind of maturity in Christ described in Romans 12, the Bible will have to be read, and appropriated."[3]

The role of the Bible in non 'Bible Study' groups

Apart from worship services the church has traditionally regarded the detailed study of the Bible in the local Christian community as the province of the mid-week Bible study group. If, however, the Word of God is concerned with life, abundant life, then Bible study should not be confined to the Bible study groups *per se.*

During the past two decades, the church has seen many new types of groups spring up such as: fellowship groups, growth groups, prayer cells, sharing groups, koinonia groups, etc. All have the same basic goal of growing together into the likeness of Christ through the community of love and support that we are called to share in Jesus' Spirit. In many cases such groups have replaced the traditional Bible study meeting. However, even where specific Bible study may not be a primary objective of such groups I personally would stress the value of some form of regular Bible study. For any group to grow, it requires some objective task outside its own life. The Bible very readily fulfills this need.

Although study of other Christian books can be very valuable, the experience of the church throughout the centuries has shown that through the Bible God can more effectively address and change human lives than through any other book. In some mysterious way, the Bible is "in-breathed" by the Spirit of God and that Spirit is "out-breathed" into our lives as we submit ourselves to Him ("inspired" literally means "God-breathed") making us new creations, maturing us in the knowledge and way of Jesus and leading and equipping us for God's mission of reconciliation in the world.

Five ways of looking at the Bible

In his stimulating book *Find Your Self in the Bible,* Karl A. Olsson outlines five ways of looking at the Bible. Firstly, one may look at it **as mystery.** It is seen as something remotely different from the ordinary. It is holy, lifted up, something apart, detached from the everyday events in life. It has no real horizontal aspect — little or no application to relationships between humans, it is exclusively vertical — concerned with our relationship with God.

Secondly, it may be viewed **as heroics,** a book of stories about unreal people. Men and women who lived halfway between heaven and earth. People who were all heroes. Not to be compared with strugglers like you and me. A third way is to treat it **as ethics.** Those who have this perspective, view it as rules and regulations, moralistic, a book of laws to be obeyed. Jesus came into headlong collision with the religious leaders of His day who took this stance. It produces the critic, the judge, the idealist. Grace finds a minor place in this philosophy.

To look at it **as theology** is a fourth manner of seeing the Bible. Here it is treated as an object of enquiry, a criterion of intellectual purity. Its study is limited to the professional. Such a position can restrict the Bible from having much to do with life and faith.

The fifth way Olsson suggests we can look at the Bible is to see it as **miracle.** It is the record of God's mighty and miraculous acts in dealing with people who were deeply conscious of their humanity. It clearly sets forth God's grace, His undeserved favour of love dealing with these people. It is a book about life and faith, concerned with personhood and every dimension of relationships both vertical and horizontal. The last of these ways of looking at the Bible is obviously the approach which will most likely lead to transformation in the lives of those studying it.

There are a number of ways a group could plan to get to grips with the Bible:

1. *Get an overview of the Bible as a whole.* Small groups have not always had a good model of Biblical studies. Generally Bible study has been too piecemeal. There is a need for a good overview of the Bible, to study it as a complete unit rather than in the fragmented way it has been studied. This is a large undertaking and obviously a verse by verse study can't be undertaken within the group. The speed with which the study moves will vary from book to book but it is important to avoid getting bogged down or on the other hand, not capturing the main message of a particular book. Generally the group members contract to read a certain number of chapters, or a whole book in between meetings. Some will want to do their own reading of commentaries on the weekly segments.

In one group we accomplished a brief bird's eye view of the Bible in four months. This was too rushed although the majority found some benefit in it. Other groups have taken twelve months and longer. One group used Webb Garrison's *A Guide to Reading the Entire Bible in a Year,* another *The Unfolding Drama of the Bible* by Bernhard Anderson. William Barclay's book *Introducing the Bible* is a helpful background book which could be studied by itself over a brief period or in conjunction with a textual study.

The Bethel Series prepared by the Adult Christian Education Foundation in Madison, Wisconsin, U.S.A., is one of the most thorough adult Bible programmes I have encountered. After an initial orientation course for the pastor, teacher-trainees in the local parish are involved in a study course for 2½ hours each week over a period of two years, under their pastor's leadership, before they begin teaching. Adult groups are then led by these lay leaders in weekly one-hour meetings. The 40 lesson course consists of six, seven-week sessions, spaced over a two year period. People's need for this type of overview of the Bible is borne out by the participation of over 700,000 in this programme since its inception a few years ago.

Many Christians complain that they don't know what

the Bible is all about. Innovative ways of helping people get a broad panorama must be developed to meet a need so many are expressing today.

2. *Work through one book of the Bible at a time.* This is a practical way to approach Bible study as it divides the Bible into manageable units. However, this has limitations in that the interrelatedness of all the books can be missed. Certainly each book stands somewhat on its own but it must be remembered that each needs to be interpreted against the backdrop of the total revelation which the Bible gives of the nature and purposes of God. Something of the original purpose of the book can be discovered, as background information on the historical context in which the book was written is given.

   Many groups have worked through a book verse by verse by using commentaries and moving at their own speed. Others have found it more helpful to have a plan to follow covering a section of the book for one session. This has helped prevent the group getting bogged down and has held interest for the majority. Many printed resources are available for those wishing to follow this method. A useful resource for reading a book as a whole is found in Chapter 3 of *The Bible and You* by Edward Blair (Abingdon Press).

3. *Follow a subject or theme.* This can be planned by use of a Concordance, a Topical Bible or a Bible Dictionary. An authoritative resource book should also be used in conjunction with the textual study. The wealth of prepared resources available obviates the need to prepare your own studies. However, there is an advantage for a leader with some skills in Bible study to undertake the considerable research and planning required himself. Where the participants are also involved in this research it can be an enriching experience. Without willingness to do this groundwork the group can easily deteriorate into a pooling of ignorance or preconceived notions on the subject.

   The group should always make a group decision about

the subject it wishes to study. These will generally grow out of expressed needs which surface in group sharing. A question, problem or need may arise that has real meaning for the group. When the answer is sought by searching the Bible it can be a highly motivating impetus to personal study and growth.

Who should lead the Bible study?

A sensitive minister who has received specialised training in understanding the Bible and knows how to involve the group in discovering the truth for themselves can make an ideal leader. But unfortunately, many, in fulfilling their role expectations are too busy to be involved in all the groups which may benefit from their leadership. Others are not suitable because they are not of the right temperament or lack skills in leading groups. I have on a number of occasions observed men who could hold a congregation spellbound with their eloquence finding it impossible to stop fulfilling their preaching role when in a small group situation. They did not listen to others in the group and sought to preach and dominate to the detriment of the group. A wise pastor in leading a group will seek to prevent it becoming too dependent upon him. He will express his views at the appropriate time. Answers to questions will not be given by him prematurely. He will help the group probe a difficult matter to the limits of their ability first.

Most ministers can be excellent resource people for the small group because of their understanding of the Bible. A group would do well to invite their minister to provide specialist feed-in from time to time to prevent the group falling into doctrinal deviation. The Depth and Encounter Bible Study method provides for this specialised feed-in after the group has done some discovering for themselves. This also helps avoid a sharing of ignorance. A pastor who understands his role in the small group as that of enabler/facilitator will know the appropriate time to introduce material against which the group can check its findings.

A minister should be available for leaders (or members) to confer personally with him in regard to any problems that may arise out of the study group experience. There is a common fear expressed by many ministers and pastors in turning loose a small group to study the Bible without a trained person as leader.

"More than one pastor has been upset by the idea of the small group, and expressed a desire to protect his people by making sure that the only teaching they receive is "pure" teaching — from him! My response to this is to point out that this whole pattern of thinking is a return to pre-Reformation Catholicism. Luther could contend that the meanest peasant with Scripture was mightier than the greatest Pope without it — but we are unwilling to turn the Word of God over to the best educated generation of Christians the world has ever produced! Even worse, in our fear to trust the Holy Spirit to faithfully interpret His Word, we deny the Word we claim to protect for Him. For that word says "the man who really believes in the Son of God will find God's testimony in his own heart", and "the touch of His Spirit never leaves you, and you don't really need a human teacher. You know that His Spirit teaches you all things." (1 John 2:27).

"When Paul established churches he left them to God, with only the Word he taught and wrote. And God was faithful. God taught them, and they grew strong. How tragic if we can no longer trust God: if **we** insist on teaching them. No wonder today we are weak, no wonder we need renewal!

"This does not mean that a group will be deserted once it has been launched. Or that there is no role, as counsellor, for the church leadership. It does mean that development of a strong, ongoing life requires that church leadership trust God and the group and that group learn to trust God and each other."[4]

Although the leader need not be an expert it will be an asset if the leader seeks to improve his knowledge and understanding by undertaking some training in the actual study of the Bible and methods of study and teaching. Personal study of the Bible is an essential pre-requisite for the leader to bring a sharing of his personal encounter with the Word of God to the group. The lay leader should also be aware of the many helpful resources available to aid in preparation and for the group to check out their own findings.

A list of qualifications for the leader whether lay or clergy are given in "Studying the Bible in Small Groups" (Adult Leadership Leaflet — United Presbyterian Church in the U.S.A.).

"What kind of leadership is needed?

— Not the expert who has the right answers.
— Rather a person with an inquiring mind:
    — who wants to learn and help others to learn
    — who appreciates the contribution each can make
    — who has some skill in enabling him to make it.

— As a study leader he is:
    — sceptical of the easy answer
    — intolerant of the half-truth
    — accurate regarding facts and data.

— As a Bible study leader he seeks for himself and others in the group an understanding of the good news of God.
    — Helps group plumb the depths rather than merely share surface observations.

He is humble, reverent, teachable."

Principles for understanding a Bible passage

(a) Use a readable and reliable translation — e.g. the *Revised Standard Version* the *New English Bible,* or the *Jerusalem Bible*. Paraphrases of Scripture such as *The Living Bible*, while having some value, are not recommended for serious Bible study.

(b) Look for the relation of the passage being studied to its context and interpret the passage in the light of God's full revelation in Jesus Christ.

(c) Look not only for what is being said but how it is being said. Do we have straightforward matter-of-fact statements about people, their actions and words? This may be history, prophecy, or law.
Or are the statements couched in highly symbolic language — in poetry or prose? (Daniel, Revelation, Mark 13, Isaiah 24).
Is the narrative written in straightforward language, but meant to be taken symbolically? This may be parable, fable, allegory.
Or do we have sayings or discussions about morality, philosophy, theology? (e.g. Job, Ecclesiastes, Proverbs, John's Gospel, Paul's Letters).

(d) Identify the important and/or difficult words in the passage. What do they mean? (Refer to a good commentary, Bible dictionary or theological word book.)

(e) Discover the basic meaning of the passage as a whole in its historical and original setting. (Again a good commentary can help.)

(f) What is the passage saying to the individual members of the group, the group as a whole, and possibly the entire church (local and universal)? Don't be abstract or waffly here. Encourage the members to be specific and discuss in terms that will affect their individual group and church life here and now.

(g) In what ways have the members of the group found the teaching of the passage confirmed by or related to their own personal experience?

(h) To what action does God call individual members, the group and the church in the light of the passage? How can the group facilitate that action? Encourage members to share in the following session how they were able to put God's challenge to themselves and the group into practice.

Relating the Bible to life situations

The nature and mission of the Bible is transformation. Our responsibility is not merely to believe it, we are to live it. Our concern in studying the Bible is with its "experiential impact". "The eternal must relate to us in time; the objective must be made part of our subjective experience. The absolute must be absolute for me, here and now — and not merely absolute as some abstract truth "out there". The Word is to be central in the ongoing life of the small group in the church, but it is to be studied primarily to discover its impact on present experience. Unfortunately, most of us have been trained to think of and to read Scripture in terms of 'truth to be understood' rather than 'reality to live'. One problem most small groups in the church will face is tied directly to this. How can the study of the Bible be **meaningful** in our group? For this many of us will have to re-learn our approach to Scripture."[5]

Professor Ross Snyder of Chicago Theological Seminary has made a very significant contribution to this whole area of helping people discover for themselves the experiential relevance of the Bible. His Depth and Encounter Bible study method has brought a new dynamic in many groups to which I have introduced it. I consider it to be the most effective and thorough of all the many Bible study methods I have used. It can lead to new levels of communication and sensitivity in interpersonal relationships within small groups. I have seen many receive a compelling word of God through this study method and come alive spiritually or move out into new experiences of freedom and spiritual power. The full method is found on page 69. Professor Snyder writes:

"The truth of the Bible needs to get into the places where people are living. As each of us studies the Bible, an offering is being made to just one person — the reader. So when we find an important passage we should stay with it long enough to really grasp it — its core message, its feeling about life, what it can do to our own daily experiences. Too often we never stop to study precisely any particular verse, never dig and sweat intellectually or existentially; seldom become involved personally in the message of a particular passage of Scripture and, therefore, never really possess any verse. In group discussion we tend to make pious comments, knowing full well no one intends to take them seriously.

"By approaching the Bible existentially we mean the involvement of the individual in the message of a particular passage of Scripture. You ask, "What does this passage of Scripture say to me, for my life, right now?' Instead of asking, 'Why is there suffering' you ask, 'How do I react to suffering?' It's important to understand this point if Bible study is to be more than a mental exercise.

"For those for whom this line of thought about studying the Bible makes sense, we have a precise and radical method which we call 'depth' or 'encounter' study of the Bible. It is not easy. It asks that you use your mind, that you really care about the quality of the one life you have to live on this earth, that you want to investigate the live options before you.

"As you make a study, with other persons similarly interested, you can discover how profitable it is for a twentieth-century mind and a religiously serious heart to go at the Bible in company with other Christians and seekers."[6]

A major recent contribution to the study of the Bible

that combines a thorough exegesis of the text with the recognition that the Bible is concerned with persons and social transformations has been by Dr. Walter Wink, Associate Professor of New Testament at Union Theological Seminary, New York. Dr. Wink in his book, *The Bible in Human Transformation* (Fortress Press, Philadelphia, 1973), argues that historical Biblical criticism is "bankrupt", "because it is incapable of achieving what most of its practitioners considered its purpose to be; so to interpret the Scriptures that the past becomes alive and illumines our present with new possibilities for personal and social transformation" (p.2).

Not that Dr. Wink underestimates the contribution of the Biblical scholars. Rather it is because their work has so much to contribute that is valuable that he argues that it must come urgently under new management. And the new management suggested by Dr. Wink is a new approach to Bible study that remains true to the objective integrity of the text, thus enabling the student to discover the author's original intention, while at the same time providing the opportunity for the Bible to be the Word of God in facilitating personal growth and social change. This personal transformation is achieved by using a questioning technique that allows the text to lay bare the truth of our own social and personal being.

While the use of this method, which does require specialist knowledge, should be reserved for those leaders with some background education in theology, Biblical exegesis and psychology, it affirms a fundamental principle for all Bible study. That is, the need to be true to the objective meaning of the text in its original setting and so avoid speculation, plus also the importance of allowing the text to speak to our lives in a way that leads to personal growth.

Some common pitfalls

A danger which should be avoided in small group Bible study is that of taking **a purely intellectual approach.** The danger here is to merely view the passage as containing a set of doctrines or propositions and not see it as mediating God's Word that addresses our feelings, and behaviour as well as our minds.

Associated with the first pitfall is the problem of not seeing the passage related to the life of the community for whom it was originally written and also related to our experience and life in the 20th century. As has already been made clear, God's Word is concerned with living. We don't study Scripture in an abstract, intellectual fashion that is little more than a philosophical discussion of correct doctrine. Bible study must be speaking to the pains and joys we experience as human beings and as Christians, and on living out Christ's Gospel in our age.

The opposite extreme to the purely intellectual approach to Bible study is the danger of **simply sharing ignorance.** If Bible study is merely subjective we fail to move beyond the feelings, attitudes and opinions of the group. While the subjective dimension is necessary, effective Bible study also demands that we come to grips with the findings of reliable scholars and teachers and understand the Bible passage in its historical and theological setting. We can overcome the dual dangers of an imbalanced subjectivity and sharing of ignorance in a number of ways:—

(i) Using a resource person to provide necessary historical, linguistic and theological background information — e.g. your minister, a Bible teacher or a well read lay person.

(ii) Providing printed resources for the group to use (e.g. commentaries, Bible dictionaries, guided Bible studies with explanatory notes).

(iii) Having one or more members of the group research beforehand possible areas requiring specialist feed-in, discover the necessary information and introduce it to the group at the appropriate time.

(iv) Record during the meeting matters requiring specialist information and at the end of the session invite members to research the various areas and share their findings at the next meeting.

By using a variety of these means learning can be stimulated. In the main it is probably a good idea to use group research to discover needed information and periodically invite a specialist to the group to discuss problem areas and through discussion with him, reinforce the discoveries the group has made.

A person does not have to be a scholar to read and study the Bible with understanding. But anyone who desires to take the Bible seriously will also need to take advantage of what others have learned. The findings of scholars can open the treasures of the Bible to those of us who do not have the technical training and commitment to do our own hard research. Don't fall into the trap of thinking that the findings of scholars are not important. Seek to use the fruits of scholarship without being burdened with the jargon and the methods of technical scholarship.

Superficial treatment of the passage is another potential problem. This danger is particularly acute if the group does not realise the importance of serious Bible study, is uncommitted to their task and to one another or fails to use a commentary or other specialist help. The problem can also arise if you try to cover too much material in one session. It is usually best to limit the group to a passage with a reasonably self-contained unit of thought — about 15-20 verses for a 1½-2 hour session. The natural paragraph divisions in the RSV are generally a useful, quick guide. However, the leader will need to exercise his own discretion. For example most groups would want to move fairly quickly through the genealogy section in Matthew 1 (although for certain specialist Bible students there is a lot that can be learned from that chapter). If the leader refers to one or two commentaries before the meeting he will find guidance regarding the optimum number of verses to cover in one session.

One further common pitfall is **failure to study the passage in its immediate context** and from the standpoint of God's full revelation in Jesus Christ in the light of the whole New Testament. A number of parts of the Old Testament for example are "sub-Christian" (e.g. "an eye for an eye and a tooth for a tooth" law). Whilst such passages must be seen in their original historical setting, we must look beyond them to God's fuller revelation of Himself and His will which we find in the New Testament. Also difficult or ambiguous passages in the New Testament must be interpreted in the light of what is clearly shown elsewhere in the Bible as God's will as revealed through Christ in His earthly life or through His Spirit.

Bible study in small groups has received just criticism in many cases because **it has not resulted in action.** In Bible study, we should seek to sense and then go and do, God's will. It carries with it a commitment to do God's will as He leads. We need "the freedom to be responsible". Freedom is found in obedience. The purpose of the Bible is to transform human lives and situations.

Karl Olsson's book *Find Yourself in the Bible* (Augsburg 1974) introduces us to a fresh and creative new form of Bible study. He explains that Relational Bible Study is people looking together into a mirror and finding their lives reflected. The Bible characters and situations come alive as we identify with them and read those ancient stories in the light of today's world. The Bible is seen as a book about the one thing that does not change. So long as people are people, personal relationships will remain the same. The Bible is a book of relationships, with God, with ourselves, with others and with our world. It is timeless because it concerns itself with love and hate, loyalty and treachery, fellowship and enmity — with relationships.

In Relational Bible Study we endeavour to stop making Bible characters into things or objects without basic human feelings and needs. We seek to let them live again. As we take time to listen to them and sense their feelings we will have a strange sense of identity with them. The Prodigal Son becomes me, the Woman at the Well is me, Martha is my new name and I become part of the original drama. God's message to them becomes His message to me. The same avoidance of objectivity and 'thinging' people in the Ancient Text must now apply to my relationships in the here and now with God, my fellow group members, myself and the world. Relationships are no longer avoided. The masks we have worn for so long are discarded. We interact personally. God, Others and Myself come alive. I am no longer a finished and packaged thing. God is no longer an absentee from His creation. With others we can now confess, listen, pray and relate at new and deeper levels. The world ceases to be so big that I have no responsibility for it. It is here — at my side in the form of people needing my care and concern.

Karl Olsson suggests four principles of relational Bible study. He doesn't claim they are novel or startling. They are the principles which informed homiletics have followed for so long.

"If there is any difference between conventional Bible study and what we are talking about, it lies in the manner of presentation. Relational Bible study is not something to be taught and studied. It is not a preacher or teacher giving content to students, pouring a full notebook into an empty one. It is people looking together into a mirror and finding their lives reflected. Relational Bible study is a vision of myself in relationship. Hence it leads to no programmed result. It may bring me to conversion, but it may not. It is open-ended.

1.   The first principle of relational Bible study is to **make the story my story.** This means being willing to enter into the magnetic field of the character and incidents as if they concerned me. To give myself to it, to make it my story, means that I do not have any neat little immunities. The Bible becomes me.

But to make the passage my story means that I feel not only the excitement of that long vanished scene but the deep need for Jesus and his ministry. I feel **my own need** of Him.

2.   The second principle I would suggest is that **we identify with a character in the story.** To **feel what the Biblical person feels** immediately involves relationships.

3.   The third principle of relational Bible study is to **find the gospel.** The gospel is the unbelievable truth that God thinks each one of us important enough to come to us, and is willing to trust us even though we fail Him again and again.

4.   The fourth principle is to **give the story a name.** By this I mean summing up the passage in a telling picture or metaphor. It provides a handle. Bruce Larson's Bible Study on Jesus' raising Lazarus has the title, "Unwrapping Lazarus". I have called the parable of the Prodigal Son, "Come to the Party". Giving the story a name thus does more than dress up such abstract terms as 'conversion' and 'regeneration' in figurative language. The name or metaphor makes the generalization particular and thrusts it down to a level of consciousness where flow the springs of feeling and will. It may make the hearer **want** to be unwrapped from all the hangups that wrap him, or to go to the party forever. It may make him want to be a new person and live in a new world."

In *Find Your Self in the Bible* Olsson gives a number of sample studies and helps his reader develop skills in designing his own relational studies. One has been reproduced (by permission) on page 106.

It should go without saying that any study group leader must be both committed to and prepared for his role. Part of the practical outworking of such commitment and preparation is the building up of a resource library. Such a library may be the responsibility of the group leader, the group itself, or the wider Church but in any event the library should be available to all members of the group. I would suggest that a minimum investment of $50 to $100 is essential. Some of the basic books you will need are:—

1) Bibles

It goes without saying that your basic resource is a Bible. These fall into two broad categories, standard Bibles in a variety of translations and study Bibles. My recommendation is that you have a Revised Standard Version with a centre reference (or a Jerusalem Bible with notes) and one or two modern translations for example, The Living Bible and don't overlook J. B. Phillips translation — it has a lot to commend it.

2) Commentaries

I suggest that you acquire a good one-volume commentary of the whole Bible. In addition you should have more specific individual commentaries on each book of the Bible that you are studying. There are a number of paperback commentaries available, such as Torch, William Barclay and Tyndale series. However, as the single book commentaries are of varying standard, even within a series, I suggest you seek the advice of your minister or a teacher of Biblical studies before making any specific purchase of these or the one-volume commentary on the whole Bible.

Ensure that the commentaries you choose include both the theological and historical dimension, together with a general introductory section to the book concerned. There are quite a number of commentaries available reflecting differing theological standpoints. It will be up to the leader to select what he considers to be suitable. The *Jerome Biblical Commentary,* the *New Bible Commentary* (I.V.F.), *The Interpreter's One Volume Commentary on the Bible* (Abingdon), the *One Volume Bible Commentary* by William Neil, and the new *Peake's Commentary on the Bible* (Nelson), edited by H. H. Rowley and Matthew Black; (contributors include F. F. Bruce), are the most popular.

3) **Bible Dictionaries**

Bible dictionaries give a background to the different customs, place names, characters and theological words that appear in Scripture arranged in alphabetical order. They are ideal for quick, ready reference. Popular one volume dictionaries are *Harper's Bible Dictionary* (Harper & Row) and the *New Bible Dictionary* (I.V.F.).

4) **Concordances**

These help you locate specific verses or names in the Bible. There are a number of small abridged concordances on the market but I recommend you pay the extra for one of the following: Nelson's *Complete Concordance of the Revised Standard Version* or the Cruden's *Complete Concordance of the Bible* (Authorised Version).

There are other resources you should include in your "kit" such as a Bible Atlas; background books will also be helpful such as the *Lion Handbook to the Bible,* those mentioned in this chapter and a variety of others.

Bible study and prayer

We began this chapter by referring to the Westminster Confession. After declaring that the Bible contains all that is necessary for salvation, the Confession goes on: "Yet notwithstanding, our full persuasion and assurance of the infallible truth and divine authority thereof, is from the inward work of the Holy Spirit, bearing witness by and with the word in our hearts." It further states: "We acknowledge the inward illumination of the Spirit of God to be necessary for the saving understanding of such things as are revealed in the word". Men need the Spirit to enable them to fully understand the meaning of the Word of God. Through the Holy Spirit God gives us the grace to be willing and able to put into action His revealed intention for us. In other words, study of God's Word and prayer must go hand in hand. Barclay wisely exhorts us — "We do well to approach the Bible with George Adam Smith's great prayer on our lips:

'Almighty and most merciful God, who hast given the Bible to be the revelation of thy great love to man, and of thy power and will to save him; grant that our study of it may not be made in vain by any callousness or carelessness of our hearts but that by it we may be confirmed in penitence, lifted to hope, made strong for service, and filled with the true knowledge of thee and of thy son Jesus Christ: this we ask for thy love's sake. Amen'."

References

1. William F. Barclay, *Introducing the Bible* (The Bible Reading Fellowship, 1972).
2. Charles M. Laymon, *A Handbook for Know Your Bible Study Groups* (Abingdon, 1959), pp. 9, 10.
3. Roy H. Ryan, *Planning and Leading Bible Study* (For Pastors and Lay Teachers), (United Methodist Church, Nashville, 1964), p. 1.
4. Lawrence O. Richards, *A New Face for the Church* (Zondervan, 1970), pp. 180, 186.
5. *A New Face for the Church,* p. 178.
6. Ross Snyder, from a pamphlet describing the Depth and Encounter Bible Study Method.

4   Bible Study Methods in Small Groups

In this chapter you will be introduced to Bible study methods some old and well proven; some new, from overseas or written locally, and offering real promise. Where we have been aware of the source it has been acknowledged and where possible permission gained to reproduce it. However, many of these methods have come to us in a roneoed form with no acknowledgement. We regret we have not been able to trace and recognize their origin.

In most groups it is advised to start with a method suitable to a newly formed group, for example, the Swedish Symbol Sharing or Silent Sharing Method. After one or two sessions the group can move to a deeper method of Bible study.

Most of these methods require a degree of honest sharing. If groups are content to operate behind their "masks" this lack of openness will result in little more than a "head trip" and a superficial application to life. Honesty will not come automatically and often there are barriers of in-built resistance and years of non-honest approach to sharing to be overcome. There may be awkward or difficult moments. When these arise the group must work them through with sensitivity and as a result be stronger for having faced the difficult situation. Experience from small groups that have been functioning shows that it is worth doing.

Don't over-use any one method. Vary your method as this helps to hold interest and broadens the learning experience.

Finally, be open to the Holy Spirit! Use the group as a beautiful gift from God and let it be a blessing to all the group members as well as the local church. Well-sounding words — yes, but proven in experience. Bible Study can be a vital and lively asset for the Holy Spirit, changing you for the better in a way that will influence others with whom you live and work.

BIBLE STUDY METHODS
FOR SMALL GROUPS
INDEX

1   ADAPTOYL BIBLE STUDY METHOD

This method was designed by a youth leadership conference at Dapto on the south coast of New South Wales. It is useful with a thoughtful group which has done some previous group Bible Study.

The passage to be studied should be at least 6 or more verses. Parts of the epistles and the teachings of Jesus are suitable for this method.

The four steps:

1. **Individual study of the passage** with each person using the five symbols and recording their findings. (Usually a minimum of 10 to 15 minutes is allowed — however time varies with length of passage and maturity of group).
2. **Group sharing** of their personal discovery. Each member shares their findings under one symbol before moving on to the next. General discussion is avoided to allow each member to share.
3. **General discussion** may follow. Unresolved questions are recorded for discussion in a plenary session or further study and report back.
4. **Research.** Concordances, Commentaries, Bible Dictionaries and other Bible study aids are used to help answer unresolved questions and generally extend the groups' knowledge and understanding of the passage.

 That's great! I haven't seen it that way before. This is a new thought.

 I'm hung up on this. I can't get onto what it means.

 I don't really understand this but I want to say 'yes'.
There is something about it which seems great!
I have questions or doubts about this but it moves me.

(The word for this symbol is **Interrobang**. It

is a combination of question and exclamation marks. It is the first new punctuation mark since AD 1671. It expresses the incredibility of life today. The Remington Rand Corporation have introduced it for the world of computers.)

This is not new but it comes through to me now with greater emphasis and meaning.

I feel compelled to take this seriously and this would involve . . .
(Don't generalize — be specific. Think of what situations and relationships would be affected. Keep it personal.)

WORKSHEET

SYMBOL	VERSE	COMMENTS
! THAT'S GREAT! I HAVEN'T SEEN IT THAT WAY BEFORE. THIS IS A NEW THOUGHT.		
? I'M HUNG UP ON THIS! I CAN'T GET ON TO WHAT IT MEANS.		
? I REALLY DON'T UNDERSTAND THIS BUT I WANT TO SAY "YES"! THERE IS SOME-THING ABOUT IT WHICH SEEMS GREAT. I HAVE DOUBTS OR QUES-TIONS BUT IT MOVES ME.		

THIS IS NOT NEW
BUT IT COMES
THROUGH TO ME
NOW WITH
GREATER EM-
PHASIS AND
MEANING.

I FEEL COM-
PELLED TO TAKE
THIS SERIOUSLY
AND THIS WOULD
INVOLVE . . .
(DON'T GENERAL-
IZE — BE SPECIFIC
—KEEP IT
PERSONAL).

2   ADAPTOYL RESEARCH STUDY METHOD

Developed from the Adaptoyl Bible Study Method by an Adult Study Group at Junee (in the Riverina area). The Research method gives opportunity for members to spend more time looking at the passage as a whole, as well as its individual application. This method allows for two weeks' study of the theme and the passage related to the theme.

The steps

1.   The group is broken into groups of **two** people. The groups of two then spend the allotted time **(30 mins.)** working on research of the passage. The emphasis is on gaining knowledge and/or new insights. **The findings of the two are recorded** for sharing in the larger plenary session **(20 mins.).** Each member **individually** completes the worksheet after completing the research **(10 mins.).** The time factors may fluctuate as determined by the group.

2.   At the end of the allotted time for the above work **the groups come together** for a time of **sharing their research findings only.** (This is the 20 mins. plenary session mentioned above.) No discussion of the material entered on the worksheet takes place.

3.   In the second week the large group is **divided into groups of four.** Each member shares their findings under one symbol before moving on to the next. General discussion is avoided to allow each member to share. Be careful about the element of risk in enthusiasm "dropping off" during the week's break, from having been involved in the searching of a passage and then personally applying it and leaving it until the next week for sharing with the small group members.

4.   General discussion may follow. Unresolved questions are recorded for discussion in a plenary session or further study and report back.
For the research the group will need to have at its disposal sufficient numbers of commentaries, Bible dictionaries, concordances and any relevant material to the passage and/or subject. This should be an incentive for all members to grow in Christian knowledge and not be ashamed of it.

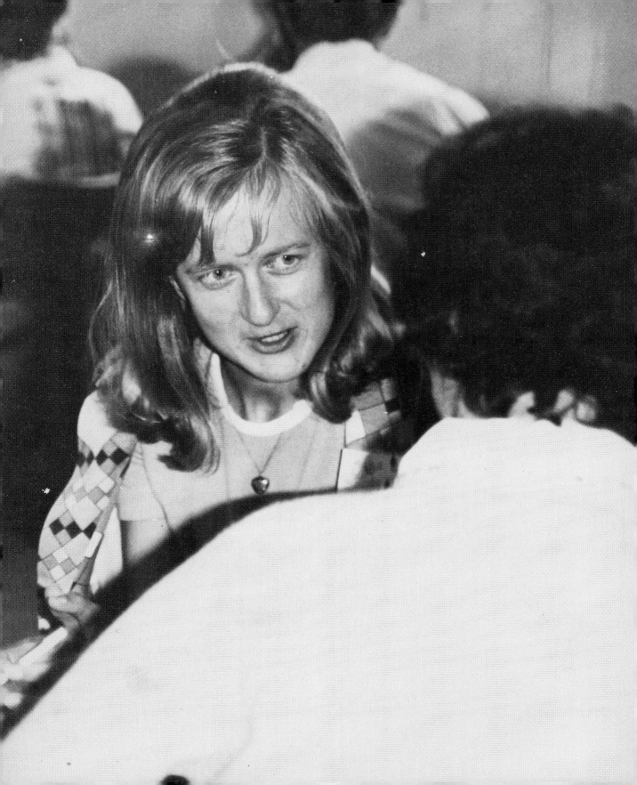

3   THE AFFIRMATION METHOD

by Douglas Parker

Individual work:

1. **Write down five points from your total life areas as a person.** They could come from your strong points or your special abilities or the positive points of your personality or things that you are exercising in the ministry to which Jesus has called you.
   For example in the teaching ministry — you may have a love for children; you may be excited about change; you may put down "patience" or "I care for others".

2. **List them with reasonable space between them.**

3. Then, away from others, before opening your Bible **ask the Lord to enable the Scripture to speak to you.** After that open your Bible at random and go through reading, scanning. If you come across a verse or passage that relates to one of your five points write it down under it or a comment on the way it strikes you, e.g. if you had "patience" and were working through St. Matthew's Gospel and came across Matthew 16:22-23 — you might write down — "Jesus was patient with Peter" or if you had "witness" as a gift and read through Acts — at Acts 1:8 you might write "we are witnesses" — we have something to share. Also jot down anything which could help in maintaining and developing your strong points.

Group work:

4. After the allotted time **get together in groups of four** (on an ad hoc basis) and then share around the group one of your five points and the way in which the Bible verse or passage related to it.

5. If they so desire **group members can respond** in a positive way to their fellow member's sharing.

6. If you still have time share a second point from each member. Responses can be made as in point 5.

7. Prayer then becomes the final part of the group work. It centres on two positive factors—
   (i) love, and
   (ii) encouragement and strength.

One person leads in prayer centring on one or both of the points shared earlier by the person on his/her left. The prayer seeks to apply one or both points of (i) or (ii) to one or both of those points.
The person on the left keeps silent as the two other members pray for him/her following the example of the member who led off in prayer.

8. Then when all three have prayed the leader touches the person on the left and he/she then leads prayer for the person on his/her left. The process is repeated so that the one who led off in prayer is the last person for whom prayer is offered.

9. One member of the group closes off with a short general prayer, thanking Jesus for the prayer time and the whole experience and commending the group's prayers to Jesus.

4   CURRENT EVENTS

This Bible Study is a good tonic for a group which is becoming too introspective and is having difficulty seeing further than themselves! The leader selects an appropriate Bible passage which is discussed in small groups (The Head, Heart and Hand method would be good here).

Each group is then given a recent newspaper and they are asked to discover in the paper any news item upon which the passage throws light. These questions may be asked:
1. Why is the passage relevant to the news item?
2. Is there something I personally could do about it? Should I be more informed? Would it be costly to my own integrity? Is there a similar situation close at hand?
3. What is the group feeling about the news item/s? Is there any action for the group to take?

Findings should be shared in a plenary session and if possible, any suggested course of action should be recorded for the group to see each subsequent week, and plans made to set it in motion.

A fitting close would be to link arms, or join hands, in a circle, symbolizing that all members are part of that decision and each has the support of the other. Each may share in prayer of commitment — either in several words or simply one word, 'yes'.

5 DEPTH AND ENCOUNTER STUDY OF THE BIBLE

by Ross Snyder

The Method in Detail

We are the kind of people who believe that each citizen should have access to the original documents of our civilization, and be able to interpret their meaning for life.

A true church is not a "little birdie in the tree" church where, periodically, little tender things open their mouths for choice morsels to drop in; the morsels that are collected by the only one who can fly — the Parson. Part of the genius of our heritage is the bringing of persons into direct encounter with the Bible — and getting it mixed up with the language they use in thinking and feeling and choosing as they live.

Whenever this has been done vigorously, there followed a generation of people who were not easily swayed by powers and principalities. Who were non-conformists in a sick civilization and in a sick church. For whom God alone was the Lord of the conscience. And in talking with one another about the meaning of the great experiences and truths found in the Bible, they created the "mind of the church" in their day, and helped establish foundations of a civilization which moved toward freedom and individual integrity and covenant with one another.

Cannot we, in our moment of history, do likewise?

If we are to create "the mind of the church" in our local congregations, we must speak to each other — out of our own experiences and the "speaking words" which are central in our conversation. But also we must speak out of the commonly accessible language of experiences and striking phrases of the Bible.

So we have a double enterprise — to dive into the depths of the Bible together, and compare what we find there and what it means to each of us.

And secondly, we must know from each other "what's stirring in you? Where do you stand? Where do you place your life? What is the statement your life makes that says

'I mean this'!"

This two-fold enterprise is what "Depth and Encounter Study of the Bible" is about.

As each of us studies a Bible verse, an offering is being made to one particular person — ourselves. So when we find an important passage, we should stay with it long enough to really grasp its core message, its feeling about life, what it can do to our expectations and experiences and journey through life. Too often we never stop to study precisely any particular verse, never sweat intellectually or let it develop existentially.* Seldom do we become involved for some time and personally in the content of a small passage of Scripture, and therefore, never really have any Bible verse that is a nucleus of life for us. And a morning star on the horizon.

First-hand interpreter

But we also need to establish life-giving imagery from the Bible as a corporate possession — until we become a group of people who believe in each other and in something together. So we must each interpret vivid parts of this basic "humankind" document to other people in such a way that they can understand it and us. And relate both to their problems and hopes. And in turn we listen to their considered interpretation and documenting from life.

Depth and encounter study of the Bible is not easy, but it is productive. It asks that you use your mind and are willing to "re-mean" your experiences. That you really care about the quality of the one life you have to live on this earth, that you want to investigate the live options before you. And do it in company with other Christians and life-makers.

Following are the steps leading into a depth and into encounters.

1.   Individual work

i.   **First, each person writes out his or her own "translation of the selected Bible passage.** The rule is that you do not use any of the words in the verse (or verses). This is often difficult to do, but we really understand a passage only when we can put it into our own words.

  This could be called, "The Bible According to John Smith", for it is the Bible put into the words John Smith

---

*By approaching the Bible existentially we mean the involvement of the individual in the message of a particular passage of Scripture. The person asks "What does this passage of Scripture say to me, for my life in some particular situation?" Instead of getting off into an abstract debate about "Why is there suffering in the world", you ask **"What has this to do with my suffering, and the suffering I cause** others?" It's important to understand this point if Bible study is to be more than chatter.

uses in his everyday experiences; into the language and imagery with which he thinks and feels and talks and makes decisions.

This language is different from the language we often find in sermons or pious advice — or the one used to write themes in high school. This is the "vernacular" — the daily, earthy language in which heavenly truth lives. The rules for the first step are:

- Write the verse as you would say it.
- Make it clear.
- Say it directly and with force.

You are not writing a sermon on the text, but "translating" the text. What you write will be about the same length as the original verse(s).

ii. **Having written the Bible passage in your own words, you now ask yourself, What would happen if I took this seriously?**

Would I see certain persons and situations — the world — any differently? See and feel about myself and my actions in a fresh new way?

Would I do anything differently?

What would I care for?

You need not write this out. Just jot down one or two ideas that come into your mind.

It usually takes from fifteen to twenty minutes to translate a verse and to do some serious thinking about it.

2. Group work

For the sharing and development of each person's thought it is best to divide into groups of five people. Each person, in turn, is given the opportunity to share. First one person (a) gives a translation and his or her thoughts on "What would happen if I took this seriously?" Then, in conversation, (b) explains some of the experiences and thoughts out of which this thinking came. Finally, together, the group (c) helps the person to develop his or her thinking. They do not criticize or pass judgment. They do not react to a person's offering as being "good" or "bad". For each person the most important translation for his or her spirit's growth is the one which he or she makes. The group may help the person test his or her thinking by asking questions such as, Now how would you apply that to this kind of situation (state the situation)? What would you say to this idea (state the idea)?

First it is important to receive one individual's thoughts and concern, and for at least one or two persons in the group to state what has been communicated to them. The person being received is then given an opportunity to add to or correct what the others understood from what he or she has said.

Receiving the thoughts and concerns

The second important step is to help the person grow, or develop an idea, but still keep it as his or hers.

After each person in the group has been so received a general discussion on whatever has been awakened in the group is profitable.

The value of this method of Bible study lies in the distinctive way we carry on the discussion. Note that the method of sharing is different from the usual methods of group discussion where everyone jumps right in with his idea. With this approach we are meeting one another where each of us lives. Our purpose is to help each one of us become clearer in his grasp of Christian truth. We are after development, not debate.

If members of the group plunge in immediately with a "This is the way I translated it —" the more vocal people will tend to dominate, the depths of each person may never be revealed, and the members of the group may not learn the difficult art of creatively listening to another person. Furthermore, we are not being trained in our own translating and contemplation of the Bible.

A sense of group possession is made possible by the small groups coming together into one large group for fifteen to twenty minutes. Ask if someone in each group would like to have everyone hear his translation. Then ask the groups to share the issues raised so that they can be discussed profitably in the larger group.

Learning how to participate in such an encounter with the Bible and one another is difficult; therefore it is wise for a leader to work with one group of five persons for three or four sessions before attempting this method of Bible study with a large group. (Without a doubt this method

Working with larger groups

is best adapted to a small group eager to get somewhere with Bible study.) If you work first with one group of five there will be persons present in the larger group who will know what is to be done and how.

The method can be demonstrated with two people and a leader before a large group. In this case, the preliminary individual work is done ahead of time. Or, after everyone has made their translation, two people are used to demonstrate the method of receiving a person.

It is possible to teach the method this way to a large group: After the translations have been written out, the leader states that time will be taken for the reading of individual translations in order to learn what the verse has said to each one, and to see if the group can get its meaning. The behaviour of the leader in receiving and nurturing the translations and remarks helps everyone to learn how to carry on a thoughtful encounter. Then the group moves into examining and weighing. "What if we took this seriously?"

To sharpen this part of the discussion the leader can assume the role of a sceptic — a representative of the world. He does so by deliberately taking opposing positions and describing crucial, real-life situations so the group meets in a head-on collision with the way the world is. This will prevent the tendency to accept easy solutions. You are interested in a searching, not a surface exploration of Biblical truth.

The leader can offer his or her own "translation" and "so what" wherever it seems most relevant in this discussion. The leader takes care not to give his thinking as a "final" answer.

3. The specialist

After your group has had a few sessions on a portion of the Bible, bring in a specialist in the Bible. Have this person explain the meanings of the key Greek or Hebrew words in the passages, and help the group grasp, somewhat dramatically, what this chapter meant to the people who first heard it. This might require digging into the history of the time, the inner world of people living then, the social and religious conditions to which the passage was addressed, and the core of its message in the light of the total Christian heritage.

Then ask the specialist to share what excitement this passage arouses in him or her (not advice to other people on what they should do).

Keep clear how this differs from inviting a Bible expert to come in to lecture and then, after this person has told the group what to think, having the group discuss what has been said.

Digging on your own

In the absence of a special Bible teacher, consult such volumes as *The Interpreter's Bible* (Abingdon Press). Dig the material out for yourself. Caution: Do not go to the reference until you have come at the Bible directly with your own life, and your group has back of them three or four solid sessions.

During a period of Bible study such as we have outlined here, a person — or the whole group — may find a passage that is particularly meaningful. This meaning could then be put into the form of a litany or a meditation — further symbolizing its depths in beautiful and compelling form. A member might be given the privilege of preaching on it, adding a personal testimony of his or her understanding of the words of old.

WHAT MAKES THIS "ENCOUNTER" STUDY OF THE BIBLE

To "encounter" is to meet another person in such a way as to discover where both of you stand.

In terms of "encounter", the primary purposes of this method of Bible study are—

1. to meet the Holy Spirit as he communicates to us through the words of the Bible.
2. to encounter ourselves — to become present to ourselves as we are and are meant to be.
3. to meet — in honesty and freedom — the depths of the other persons in our group and to do so in such a way as to help each of us grow.

As with all human events, "encounter" does not always happen right away. But over a period of time it does. And these moments become a part of the treasures of our lives.

WHAT MAKES IT "DEPTH" STUDY?

It is depth study, first of all, to the degree that it helps a person to put into words the vague stirrings of his or her spirit that normally do not have a chance to occupy a person's centre of attention. Until we think and talk these stirrings into some kind of symbols (words, described experiences, images of ourselves in the world) we do not possess them. We are not present to our own experiencing. And until these symbolized stirrings of the spirit are at the centre of our attention, their significance never seeps down through all our life. Only in some such kind of thinking and talking with a friendly, receiving group will a person be able to possess his or her deeper experiences and awakenings.

Secondly, it is depth study to the degree that a ministry of relationship is going on at the same time that the study is going on. Deep calls unto deep. Some depths of human existence are experienced only in the I-Thou mode of meeting. Whenever we come out with an experience or personal hope that is meaningful to us, and our offering is received with understanding but not treated with softness, we are in the presence of the holy.

Thirdly, it is depth study to the degree that we go down through the levels of penetration into the Bible.

At the most obvious level, there are the words of the English translation which we read. Underlying these words are certain tremendous experiences and visions of the world — the words and sentences emerged out of these experiences and visions. But underlying these are the person of the writer of this book of the Bible. It is shaking when something of the man (for example Paul or Moses) shines through to us and we unexpectedly encounter him. And finally the words, experiences, visions, and persons in the Bible sometimes become transparent, pointing to the God who is the Depth of depths.

So that our study may enter into these "levels" of the depth we search—

The **words** of the passage.
the **experiences and visions** of the world underlying the words.
the **person** who wrote the passage.
The **God** (Holy Spirit) speaking to us in the midst of our struggle and commitment.

Kinds of passages to study by this method

The suggestions given below indicate the **type** of passages which lend themselves well to this method of Bible study. On the whole, narrative passages are not so fruitful for translation. Only one verse, or one unit of verses which can be kept in mind at once, should be used. Never take a whole chapter; too many points would be glossed over.

In many instances, the passages given here would be broken up into smaller units for study. They deal with frequent problems and the offer of life which Christianity makes.

Romans 8:1-19; 12:1-2.
Ephesians 3:16-19
(Possibly selections from all of Ephesians)
Philippians 1:27-30; 2:1-13; 4:4-13
II Timothy 2:1-5; 14, 15
Hebrews 12:1-17
James 1:2-4, 19-27
I Peter 2:1-10; 3:13-17
I John 1; 2:9-11
Matthew 5:3-16
John 15:9-21; 26-27.

After you have tried this method of Bible study a few times, try selecting the key passages in a given book, and study them in order, or ask members of the group to suggest a favourite Bible verse or two for such study.

Dangers of such a method

The primary danger of this method is that we will miss the whole sweep of a book, its overall vision and message. We can concentrate exclusively on drawing fine conclusions from individual passages.

But this is not necessarily so. The protection is in the selection of verses. One method of selection is to try to study in sequence the crucial passages of a book of the Bible so that its sweep and line of argument stand out much more clearly than if one tried to study each verse or take a jet trip through the whole book at once.

One of the advantages of this method of study is that it safeguards against individual bizarre interpretations. The group discussion and the later encounter with "official" biblical interpretations provide means of self-correction. But unless people talk with other people, all kinds of misconceptions of the Bible may be held. It is, of course, impossible for the group to become so enamored of its own interpretations that it fails to consult those who have made the Bible their lifetime study.

The procedures described here may not provide enough room for doubts and questioning. They will inevitably arise in the general discussion periods; so the group should feel free to schedule a discussion on the points raised. The method, of course, ought not to become an ironclad rule. But its point is a proper one. Let's first try to be sure of what is being said in the Bible verse and what it would do to life. Then the human mind must wrestle with what is the Word of God, and what is merely a reflection of the social customs of the writer's time; for example, some of the things Paul says about women.

But let us not dwell so long upon the possible mistakes we can make that we evade picking up the Bible and going at it directly. Let us be cheered by the remark of William Tyndale, in his Prologue to the Book of Romans in his 1534 translation of the New Testament, for it also applies to the entire Bible.

> The more it is chewed, the pleasanter it is,
> and the more groundedly it is searched,
> the preciouser things are found in it.

Illustration of translation

It will be both helpful and confusing to read the "translations" other people have made in some Bible passages. But to illustrate what we have been talking about: (The following "translation" of Ephesians 4:14-15 was written by a person who had worked for a summer in a disintegrating area of a large city in the United States. It was aimed at a particular teenage boy. While it does not say all that the Bible passage does, it is in the language and experience world of the boy and speaks to him where he is in his religious development. The translation is an illustration of forceful and direct communication. However, it does approach a sermon in length, and so is more a paraphrase than a translation.)

> *That we may be no longer children, tossed to and fro and carried about with every wind of doctrine, by the sleight of men, in craftiness, after the wiles of error; but speaking truth in love, may grow up in all things into him, who is the head, even Christ (Ephesians 4:14, 15).*

"It ain't easy to be a man in this world. There's a lot of mean folks in it; folks who will do you in if they have a chance. There are others who won't give you a chance; they'll grind your face in the dirt. They don't want no part of you.

And there are friends who can get you off the beat. Sports, noise and glamour can sweet-talk you away from getting the good education you need to be yourself in this world. You can get so wound up in being a big-shot with flashy cars and clothes that you will never amount to anything.

You've got to have confidence in your own guts — but you need more than that, or else you'll not have the stuff when the chips are down. You can only say no to temptation when you know who you want to be, and what you believe to be really important.

Otherwise, you've got no defense but a big mouth and a hot head. And you'll lose out, for each of these temptations eats away at your deepest strength. You can't laugh at any of them, cause they can destroy you.

It's only you that can decide what's important to you, and how you should act. So you've got to keep hold of what you really trust, so you'll make it."

6 DEPTH AND ENCOUNTER BIBLE STUDY

A Summary

We have found it helpful to give a brief summary to groups using this method.

A. Silent prayer:

For insight — "Lord help me to grasp the meaning of this passage and enable me to express it clearly and then take it seriously".

B. Individual work:

a. Write out your own translation:

— **Pray** as you think and write.
— Try to use different words from those in the various translations as far as possible.
— Endeavour to put in your own words each of the main words before you write out your translation.
— Write it as **you** would say **it,** imagine you are writing a letter to a friend.
— Make it clear, keep it simple.

b. Ask yourself: (Do some serious thinking).

— "What would happen if I took this seriously?"
— "Would I see certain persons and situations differently?"
— Would I do anything differently?"
— "What would I care for?"

(Just jot down one or two ideas that come to mind. You won't necessarily find an answer to each question.)

C. Work group (Divide into groups of five).

N.B. These are **not** discussion groups — these are essentially opportunities to share — we will do more listening than speaking, concentrate on what people are saying, work hard at listening— love the person as he/she speaks.

a. **Each person in turn given opportunity to share:**

— Give translation and thoughts.
— Explain reason for this thinking.
— One or two persons in the group may state what has been communicated to them. The person being received is then given the opportunity to add to or correct what others understand from what he or she has said.

b. **Group:**

— Helps each person develop his or her thinking.
— Does not criticize or pass judgment.
— May ask questions (only to test thinking), e.g. "How would you apply that to this situation?" or "What would you say to this idea?"

• Help the person grow or develop an idea **but still keep it his or hers.**

• **We are after development not debate.**

c. **General discussion.** After each person in the group has been so received, a general discussion on whatever has been awakened in the group is profitable.
The value of this method of Bible study lies in the distinctive way we carry on the discussion. Note that the method of sharing is different from the usual methods of group discussion where everyone jumps right in with his ideas. With this approach we are meeting one another where each of us lives. Our purpose is to help each one of us become clearer in his grasp of Christian truth. We are after development, not debate.
If members of the group plunge in immediately with a "This is the way I translated it —" the more vocal people will tend to dominate, the depths of each person may never be revealed, and the members of the group may not learn the difficult art of **creatively listening to another person.** Furthermore, we are not being trained in our own translating and contemplation of the Bible.

D. Further suggestions

After your group has had a few sessions on a portion of the Bible, bring in a specialist in the Bible. Have this person explain the meanings of the key Greek or Hebrew words in the passages, and help the group grasp, somewhat dramatically, what this chapter meant to the people who first heard it.

Then ask the specialist to share what excitement this passage aroused in him or her (not advice to other people on what they should do).

Keep clear how this differs from inviting a Bible expert to come in to lecture and then, after this person has told the group what to think, having the group discuss what the expert has said.

In the absence of a special Bible teacher, consult such volumes as *The Interpreter's Bible* (Abingdon Press) or other commentary. Dig the material out for yourself. **Caution!** Don't go to the reference until you have come at the Bible directly with your own life, and your group has back of them three or four solid sessions.

E. Kinds of passages to study by this method

The suggestions given below indicate the **type** of passages which lend themselves well to this method of Bible study. On the whole, narrative passages are not so fruitful for translation. Only one verse, or one unit of verses which can be kept in mind at once, should be used. Never take a whole chapter; too many points would be glossed over.

In many instances, the passages given here would be broken up into smaller units for study. They deal with frequent problems and the offer of life which Christianity makes.

Romans 8:1-19, 12:1-2.
Ephesians 3:16-19.
(Possibly selections from all of Ephesians.)
Philippians 1:27-30; 2:1-13; 4:4-13.
II Timothy 2:1-5; 14, 15.
Hebrews 12:1-17.
James 1:2-4, 12, 19-27.
I Peter 2:1-10; 3:13-17; 2:9-10.
I John 1; 2:9-11.
Matthew 5:3-16.
John 15:9-21; 26-27.

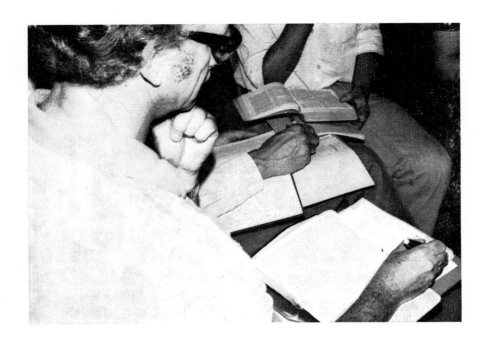

7   DEPTH BIBLE STUDY

(This is a modification of Professor Snyder's method.)

This is an approach to Bible Study for the serious reader who really seeks to grasp a given passage of Scripture, its core message, its feeling about life, what it can do to our daily experiences. It is not easy. It asks that you use your mind, that you really care about the quality of the **one** life you have to live on this earth, that **you** want to investigate the live options before you.

1.   Individual work

i   **Try to get the full impact of the passage by reading it thoroughly as a whole.**

ii   **Try to understand what the author (or speaker) is trying to communicate and why.** Attempt to understand the author:

how he feels within
what his convictions are
what he feels to be important
what he is trying to do
what is bothering him
what he is enjoying
the experiences he has had
Try to capture his inner, personal condition and concern.

iii   **Write out your own "translation" of the selected passage.** Put what is being said in your own words, as you would say it, in everyday words, phrases and imagery. A person really understands a passage only when he can put it into his own words. Write the verse as you would say it. Make it clear. Say it directly and with force. You are not writing a sermon on the text or trying to explain it, only to "translate" it. What you write will be about the same length as the original verse(s).

iv   Having written the Bible passage in your own words, **now ask yourself,**

What would happen if I took this seriously?
What difference would it make in my life?
Would I see persons and situations — the world — any differently?

Would I see and feel about myself and my actions
in a fresh new way?
Would I do anything differently?
What would I care for?

It is important here to be very specific. Do not answer
merely "yes or no"—spell out a specific instance and
think about the reason for your answer. You need not
write this out—just jot down one or two ideas that come
into your mind.

2. Group work

For the sharing and development of each person's
thought **we will divide into groups. Each person, in turn, is
given the opportunity to share.**

First, one person gives his translation and his thoughts
on "what would happen if I took this seriously?" Then in
conversation he explains some of the experiences and
thoughts out of which his thinking came. Finally, together
the group helps him develop his thinking. They do not
criticize or pass judgment. They do not react to his offering
as being "good" or "bad". The group may help the person
test his thinking by asking questions such as "Now how
would you apply that in this kind of situation?" "What
would you say to this idea (state the idea)?"

After each person in the group has been so received,
a general discussion on whatever has been awakened in
the group is profitable.

8   EIGHT QUESTIONS

This method may be **used individually or in small groups.** Each person or group is given a **sheet of paper** with the **eight questions printed** so that there are enough spaces left for writing in the answers to the questions. When all have **finished**, the **summing-up can be a comparison of all the answers** of the individuals or small groups. **If time is short** the **two most important questions are, "What is the central meaning?"** and, **"What act of obedience follows?"**

Preparation required:
a.   A copy of the questions for every person or each group. If working with one group, the questions may be placed on a chalkboard and blank sheets of paper issued.
b.   A chalkboard or substitute will be needed for summarising.

The eight questions:
1.   What are the scenes?
2.   What are the difficult words? (Either because we do not understand them or they have been used so often they have lost their full meaning.)
3.   What is the relation of this passage to the whole context in which it occurs?
4.   Why is it in the Bible at all?
5.   What is the central meaning? (Ask what does the passage say about God and His attitude to us, about our attitude to Him and about our attitude to each other.)
6.   Can you illustrate this central truth from the History of the Church, and especially from the life of the Church today?
7.   What is the meaning of this passage for our own group today? How does it affect the content of our faith? Our prayer life?
8.   What act of obedience follows from this, for the Christian community and for each of us individually?

Passages suitable
for this method
- The Parable of the Great Supper. Luke 14:15-24.
- The Raising of Lazarus. John 11:38-44.
- Jesus and the Accusing Pharisees. Matt. 15:1-20.

9   ENCOUNTER AND ENABLE

Adapted from Lyman Coleman's Depth Study Method

Purpose: To deal with the basis for a certain subject from the viewpoint of Scripture and to share the results with each other in small groups.

Setting: Informal groups of four, sitting on the floor or in chairs that can be moved close together.

Time required: A minimum of 60 minutes, plus a free period at the close for groups who need a little more time.

Materials required: A pencil and workbook for everyone.

Procedure
(1) **preliminary exercise** — with each person working on his own.
(2) **small-group interaction** — with everyone belonging to a small group of four.
(3) **depth encounter** — with everyone staying in his small group.

The leader of the group should be prepared to explain the instructions in his or her own words, giving examples from his or her paraphrase and application in order to set the pace for honesty.

Preliminary exercise (15 minutes)
1. **In silence, read over the Scripture passage for the session,** pausing after each verse to **jot in the margin** one of the following symbols:

If you understand the verse clearly.

If you have a question about the meaning.

If you get special inspiration from the verse.

If you really get convicted about something in your life. (Spot on!)

86

You can draw more than one symbol for each verse, but you must have at least one for each verse.

2. **Ask yourself the question, Which two verses speak to my need or my situation? Underline** them.

3. Then, in the top-left corner of the worksheet, write the number of the **first verse you have chosen** and draw a circle around it.
Read the verse again, and starting with the first part, **rewrite it in your own words.**
You may want to rewrite the first verse two or three times, each time going a little deeper into the meaning as you see it.
Then, go a step further and **think of the verse in terms of your own situation at school,** at work, at home or at church. Try to include in your paraphrase what the verse really means in the situation where you live.

4. When you have finished with the first verse you underlined, write the number of **the second verse** you underlined and put a circle around it. Then, proceed to **rewrite this verse in your own words in the same way—** expanding on the deeper meaning of the verse for your life and situation.

5. **When 10 minutes are up,** regardless of whether everyone is through with his paraphrase, **move on to the application.**
Ask yourself the question, **As far as these two verses are concerned, what is the thing I must work on in my life?** It can be anything from a bad attitude at work to a broken relationship with your wife, but it should be honest and specific — very specific.
Whatever comes to mind as the need in your life at the moment, jot it under the word **Application** at the bottom of your work sheet. It does not have to be long. Just a few words will do, such as 'screaming at the children'!
Then, **under the need put down three things you can do about it during the next week.** If 'screaming at the children' is the problem in your life, you might jot down: Tell them I am sorry when I scream at them. Ask their help. Commit the problem to God.
After a couple of minutes, the leader will call "time" and ask you to move into small groups.

Small-group interaction (30 minutes)

1. Gather together **in groups of four** and have one person in each group serve as the **moderator.** This person's task is to see that the discussion stays on the subject and the material is covered. The role of moderator should rotate to a different person at each session.

2. The moderator asks **each person** in the group **to explain which verses he or she picked for his paraphrase — and why.** (The 'why' will be interesting in itself.) Then **those who have paraphrased** the first verse in the passage **read aloud what they have written.** As each paraphrase is read, the **moderator should listen for something that would be good for "gut level" discussion.** The moderator can then come back with a question that focuses the discussion on this area. For instance, Bill, what did you mean by "uptight"? or, Helen, would you mind giving me an example out of your own experience to clarify what you mean?

3. After **four or five minutes move on to the next verse** that has been paraphrased and do the same.

4. Follow this procedure verse by verse through the passage until all of the verses that have been paraphrased have been covered — or until the 30 minutes are up.

Depth encounter (15 minutes)

1. In the small groups **each person in turn shares his application,** explaining the thing he wants — needs — to work on his life and what he is going to do about it.

2. **After the sharing, gather together and form a circle of love.** In oneness and dependence, **pray specifically for each other,** using the first person, I . . . me . . . my.

3. When your small group is finished, dismiss yourselves and slip out quietly without disturbing the groups that are still meeting.

10   HEAD — HEART — AND HAND

This is another method of Bible Study which is comprised of three distinct phases.

HEAD: Here **the facts** about the passage are discovered — the meaning of the words — build-up of the story — context — for what, to whom, by whom it was written — what kind of people were they — what were their needs, etc. **This may be done by the leader verse by verse or by the group using one of the previous methods.**

HEART: The group as a whole is divided into **small groups** so that all may have the opportunity to share. **The passage is read silently** and **each individual tries to find** the **heart** of the **passage** (central meaning) for himself or herself that day. (The Silent Sharing Method may be used here.)

HAND: This phase deals with **ACTION.** Here care should be taken that the group ACTS either as a group or as individuals. The leader accepts **reports from the "Heart"** groups, summing up as they are presented to the group as a whole to give an overall picture of what has been discovered. For a few minutes these **findings are discussed** to find which is **the most important one for the group** (although individuals may make their choices as well).

ACTION often falls into three sections:
a.   **Some obvious group action** for the group, Church or community.
b.   If there is a **feeling** that the **group needs to know more, further study may be planned.** (Make sure that this doesn't become an escape route.)
c.   **Individuals decide themselves** on the things which need to be changed in their lives or attitudes or outlook.

Preparation required:
a.   Have the smaller groups ready so that time will not be lost here. Each group needs a competent leader.
b.   Provide paper and pencils for each member of the group.
c.   Each person will need his Bible for the second phase of the study.
d.   Materials for reporting and charting findings from the groups will be needed.
e.   Enthusiasm to see this method through to its conclusion is needed.

Example of this method:
• A Changed Life in a New Society—Colossians 3:1-17.

11 HUMAN NEED AND CHRISTIAN ACTION

STEP 1: The leader, or member of the group, presents an actual situation of human need. This may be in the form of suffering through a crisis, a neighbour's difficulties, a problem at work, a situation in the church, or in the town/suburb. It is flexible but needs to be specific.

Step 2: The problem having been set before them, small groups of four or five discuss the situation with what Christian insight they have. To quote William Barclay "one needs to get inside the skin of another person to see what they see and experience what they feel." This is what the members are asked to do — to study each person — not only the apparently 'wronged' person or the one suffering misfortune — but each one, in order to see the situation from every angle. After half an hour, the leader (or member leading) records the reports on a chart but makes no comment on them.

Step 3: The groups are now given a Bible passage which has been selected beforehand by the one leading, and chosen because of its relevance to the topic — only now is the Bible used. Another half hour at least is needed for this. With this passage are the following questions:—

(i) Having looked at the passage, is there anything there which prompts us to change the thoughts we had earlier? Are there any guidelines which may help decide what action to take either as (a) individuals, (b) the group, (c) the church community?

(ii) From what we have learnt in the Bible passage and the situation presented to us, what should we include in our prayers of (a) confession, (b) thanksgiving, (c) Petition.

Step 4: Reassemble in the large group and share findings. Only now, can the one leading the group make any contribution.

Step 5: Determine any action to be taken.

Step 6: Close in time of group prayer using the points which have come from Step 3. Leader to finish.

12   HUMAN TRANSFORMATION METHOD

This Bible Study is an adaptation of the procedure outlined by Dr. Walter Wink, Associate Professor of New Testament at Union Theological Seminary, New York, in his book, *The Bible in Human Transformation*. This method requires the leader to have some background theology and Biblical exegesis.

Phase 1 — Leader's preparation

Before the study group meets, the leader prepares a thorough exegesis of the passage. Based on this exegesis the leader then prepares a carefully thought out series of questions to guide the group into a greater awareness of the historical and theological background and meaning of the passage.

Phase 2 — Analysis

By means of the questions prepared by the leader, the group analyses the account, working together on their own exegesis of it. The leader may need to provide some specific technical information or guide the group when they seem bogged down or headed in the wrong direction. Questions may be asked also concerning the recording of the incident — for example — does it appear in any other gospel; do the accounts differ; why; what is the meaning of certain words, traditions, etc.

Phase 3 — Picturing the passage

The aim is now to enter more deeply into the story. By means of historical imagination, and using the critical analysis of Phase 2 as a check on sheer speculation, the passage is thought through again and members are asked to seek to relive the passage. In this phase, questions (for example) concerning what the early church understood about the nature of God and His relationship with man or who Jesus is etc, may be raised as a direct result of information from this section. If questions from this phase are factual, then the danger of premature self-reflection which fails to allow the unexpected and "offensive" elements in the text to confront the group, may be avoided.

Phase 4 — Putting yourself in the picture

In this phase the leader uses questions to help the members closely identify with the characters in the Gospel story. The members are helped to use these ancient characters as mirrors of their own lives. It involves imagination, serious thinking and honesty. The leader will need to set the pace by modelling this openness, application and deep involvement. The leader will need to avoid manipulating people into going further than they are really prepared to go in making bare their souls.

Transformation can take place during this phase. The members may hear the voice of God and feel the power of the Holy Spirit in a way similar to those who experienced a transforming encounter with Christ in the original story.

Questions based on the story of Mark 3:1-6 (for example) could go like this:

— What is your "withered" or "crippled" hand? In other words, what aspects of ourselves do we identify in this character? (Allow a short pause for people to reflect and gather their thoughts.)
— What's the pharisee in you?
— Is there a sabbath day in your life? A special part of your life that you keep for yourself? A part that you refuse entry to the work of the Spirit of God?
— Why then doesn't your "pharisee" want your "crippled hand" healed or want God to work in your "sabbath"?
— What then is the relationship between the pharisee and the crippled hand in your life?
— How does Jesus fit into the picture?
— How can Jesus relate to our pharisees, sabbaths and withered hands?

(The session in our example ends in prayer with the members reaching out to God for their various needs, and at the same time supporting one another in prayer — the conversational prayer method could be effectively used here.)

Phase 5 — Creative expression

In this concluding segment each member is asked to creatively express some aspect(s) of the passage studied. This may be done using poetry, crayons, paints, clay, etc. in the members' free time between sessions and brought to share with the group at the next meeting.

13 INDUCTIVE BIBLE STUDY METHOD

By asking the simple questions of 'how', 'when', 'where', and 'why' when looking at a Bible passage, a direct discovery of the meaning may be accomplished.

The aim of this method is to find out what the passage means, using varied resources and then, following discussion, to apply the new knowledge and insights gained to daily living and to establish a course of action to follow.

The leader's responsibility

1) To arrange for resource books such as Bibles, concordances, commentaries, maps and Bible dictionaries to be provided.

2) Prepare for each group and set the questions which are to be studied while the groups examine the passage:
   a) What is the message the author is trying to communicate?
   b) At what time was it said?
   c) Where is the author saying it?
   e) To whom is the passage addressed?
   f) What tone and expression does the author use?

3) Divides the group into small groups to research for answers to the above questions by using the available resources. Individual groups may be given a specific assignment.

4) To be prepared to give assistance if necessary.

5) Request reports from each small group and make a summary of the material.

6) Suggest areas for further study or lead the group to discover any course of action to follow.

7) Evaluates the group's learning experience.

The group members

1) Share in making the decision of which Bible passage is to be studied.

2) Clarify their goals.

3) Reflect on the questions given to them.

4) Search for the answers.

5) Record the information and report it to other group members.

6) Make special note of new ideas and information.

7) Ask what the passage means to them personally.

14   "IONA" METHOD

IN BRIEF:
1. **Small groups up to ten** including leader.
2. **Silent reading and consideration of passage** for up to ten minutes.
3. **Individual comments or queries.**
4. **General discussion.**
5. **Leaders sum up.**

PREPARATION:

The passage of Scripture to be studied is selected and reproduced on sheets of paper, preferably from a modern translation. Other versions could, of course, be referred to as desired, but the main purpose is that discussion should proceed on the basis of all participants considering and speaking about the same words. The use of the sheets also makes possible the marking of the passage, notations, recording of questions, etc.

The leader or leaders may decide to prepare a question aimed at drawing out the relevance of the passage in some particular way. If this is done, the question should be reproduced on the sheet together with the passage.

However, it would probably be more appropriate in most instances to proceed with the general purpose of **ascertaining the relevance of the passage to Christians today.**

INDIVIDUAL WORK:

The group leader distributes copies of the passage to the members, who are asked to read silently and to consider what significance the passage is seen to have. They could also be invited to note any parts of the passage, the meaning of which is not clear.

GROUP WORK:

Individual sharing

After the stipulated time, the leader invites each member in succession round the group to share his or her thoughts on the passage, and to mention any difficulties. Each person is given the opportunity to speak or not to speak as desired and there should be a permissive climate to enable this to be done. No one should be put "on the spot". The whole group should keep a brief record of comments or questions to facilitate later discussion.

It is important that all members should have their opportunity to comment on the passage **before** general discussion begins. For example, if one member disagrees with another's comment, there is a natural tendency to "leap in" and say so. However, there may be a number of side effects; firstly, that the discussion gets off on a false trail; secondly, that the discussion may preclude other members from making their initial contribution (they get forgotten); or thirdly, members who still have to make their contribution may "clam up" if they see what is happening to another unfortunate commentator.

General discussion

After the individual contributions have been received, general discussion proceeds.

ROLE OF THE LEADER:

Once general discussion begins the appointed leader may be on the same basis as the other members for some time; each is free to contribute. There may be situations, however, where it will be necessary to recall the group to the real issue involved. As appropriate, the leader may refer to individual comments made earlier, or refer to difficulties expressed.

In this regard it would be desirable, particularly in a new group, for the comment or question to be mentioned anonymously. For example, if Bill Smith has made a statement which is in error, it would be preferable to say "It was suggested earlier that such and such" rather than say "What do you think about Bill Smith's statement that such and such". Where the former method is used, it is the **idea** that tends to be discussed. With the latter method, the **person** tends to come under critical review.

The leader may conclude the session by an appropriate summing up.

It is apparent that the leader will need to be just as thoroughly prepared for study along these lines as he or she would in the situation where a leader would take a much more active or directive part. In fact, the leader needs to be much more aware of possible misapprehension and difficulties because they will tend to find freer expression.

GENERAL COMMENTS ON METHOD:

The following are comments made by persons participating in the use of the Iona method:—

Leader must be well prepared.
Leader must recognize personalities and their needs.
Encourages participation—everyone gets opportunity to speak.
Brings out all kinds of questions.
No "set" question allows discussion of group's common experiences.
Timing must be watched.
All questions not always answered.
Relationships within group improve with familiarity of method.

15   KEY WORDS

Select a passage of Scripture, and ask individual members to read through the portion several times, underlining words which recur. Compare the words in different translations, making notes of those which are changed in other versions. When the list has been compiled, the group then moves on to discuss the meaning of these words in the context in which they occur and the significance of them in relation to the daily life of the Christian.

If there is a Greek or Hebrew scholar who is able to give or to look up the words in the respective dictionaries, the search will be even more fruitful. A theological word book of the Bible is most helpful.

Some suitable passages: Matthew 5:1-13
John 10:1-18
I John 4:7-12.

16   THE MEDITATIVE USE OF SCRIPTURE

(Based on a session led by Rev. Gordon Cosby of The Church of the Saviour, Washington, D.C., at the Vineyard Retreat Centre, Louisville, Kentucky, U.S.A.)

Introduction

God speaks to us through the natural order and through people who touch our lives. He speaks most clearly and fully through the Scriptures.

The meditative use of Scripture is one of the most important ways in which the Christian is addressed by God.

It is an art which needs to be developed. It is not study, nor is it merely reading — **it is letting Christ address us.**

The purpose

The whole purpose of this experience (and indeed all our devotions) is to help us hear our destiny and to fulfil it. However, it is easy to develop devotional life apart from mission.

The question which is ever before us in true meditation is, "What is God's call on my life now?" That call will have certain characteristics:—

    (a)   There is a feeling of ultimacy — a feeling of being dealt with by God.

    (b)   There will be a feeling of impossibility — a tendency to brush if off as seeming ridiculous. On the other hand, don't miss it because is seems so simple.

    (c)   There will be a persistency — it will keep coming to you if you are continuing to be a growing person.

Change will take place within us as the Holy Spirit takes hold of this event. Growth takes place with this type of day by day encounter with the living Christ. What transforms life, making it spiritually vital and dynamic is the cumulative power of the Word of God.

THE METHOD:

The whole of the **individual work** is undertaken in **complete silence.** (We usually break silence to not allow God to get to us.)

The 4 steps:

(1) Preparing a. **Select a passage.** Each person selects their own. Ask for the guidance of the Holy Spirit as you read. Let Him select the passage which you need most at the moment. Open the Bible at random (some will find it more helpful to begin in the Gospels) and read on until a passage captures your attention.

b. **Select a very brief passage.** Sometimes it will only be a phrase. We want to encounter it at depth — a long passage won't permit this in the time we have available.

c. **Pray.** Ask that you may be personally addressed by God through this Scripture. Pray for the guidance of Scripture. Ask **for** courage to meditate upon it, for this is a dangerous business — ("it is a terrible thing to fall into the hands of the living God") — it may mean being told to "go to Nineveh"!! It will be tragic if we are disobedient and costly if we obey. Pray, "Lord, I want you to get hold of me".

Use the passage "not as a model for morality but as a mirror for our identity" (Sanders).

(2) Picturing — Use your mind to picture the original event. Use your intellect and your imagination. Bring all of the past to bear upon it to help you get into the event. It will help to write notes as you proceed.

(3) Pondering — Get into conversation with Christ. He is there within you and beside you. He is in you and you in Him. Christ is talking to **you** now, listen, talk it over with Him. Ask Him questions about yourself — "what are the implications of this passage for

(4) Praying — my life?'' Jot down notes on your inner stirrings. The Scripture provides the approach for you to get in touch with the Christ Who is alive and ever present with His people.

— Hold a real conversation with God. Express real feelings not as you think you ought to feel. Don't pretend.

Write out your prayer. Record **what you say to God** in response to His word to you through the passage you have meditated upon. **Also write what you imagine God to be saying in reply.** When we are in a close relationship with a person we can closely predict what their expected response might be. God has revealed His character to us in the Scriptures. We know sufficient about Him to have some ideas concerning the replies we could expect from Him. Let it flow back and forth until you feel the dialogue has finished. Keep what you say brief and precise. What you imagine God to be saying must be consistent with His nature and intentions revealed in Scripture and supremely through the Lord Jesus Christ.

(5) Sharing — This can be done in small groups or in a plenary session. Not every member will be asked to share. Usually it is best to only ask those to share who received a real compelling word from God — something they feel is a strong "call". Only the meditation on scripture is shared.

N.B. Silence may be a problem for some because they may be afraid that a dark disturbing thing will surface or that Christ may make real demands upon them which go beyond their present level of availability to Him.

17 MESSAGE AND MEANING

This is another approach in depth Bible study. Its purpose is to let the Scriptures speak to the individual personally. Someone has referred to it as a prayerful search for the deep personal implications of the Scriptures. The ultimate question for each person involved in such study is "What does this passage say to me?"

Robert M. Cox has prepared a series of questions that can be used in making this approach. He says, "Ask the following questions of a biblical passage:

What was the person from whom this came trying to communicate?

1. What is the main idea here?
2. What is the feeling behind it?
3. What conviction is expressed?

What was its meaning for those to whom it was originally addressed?

As you consider this passage, attempt to put yourself in the situation of those for whom it was originally intended. How does it meet the need of these persons?

What meaning does this passage have for us today?

In view of man's situation in the twentieth century, what does this say to us?

What elements are common to the original situation and our current situation?

What is the meaning of the passage for me?

1. What does it require of me with regard to:
   my relationship to God?
   my relationship to other persons?
2. Am I ready to accept this now?
   Is it too demanding?
   Do I need greater spiritual maturity before I can accept it?

It is clear to the thoughtful leader that members of the group cannot ask these questions and come to an intelligent answer without first knowing the facts that a study of good introductory books to the individual books of the Bible brings to light. There is no substitute as a background to this personal approach for historical knowledge such as these studies contain. But one must not stop there. The deeper meanings of the Scriptures which depth Bible study seeks to reach are essential if the Bible is to be known as the Word of God. The Holy Spirit speaks directly to the heart when this approach is made.

In using the depth Bible study approach in this undertaking it is suggested that for each session the group select a passage of Scripture involved in the background study of the section of the book under consideration. When the historical factors have been faced and understood, the group may then turn prayerfully to these more personal questions. The results will be significant.

18   QUESTION AND ANSWER

Select a passage from the Bible. (Narrative action or biographical passages are best.) The passage should be read in sections by the whole group. **The leader** needs to have **one or two aims in mind** when guiding the progress of the discussion and **should steer the discussion so that decisive points are reached from time to time.**

Questions should be ones that make the members think, and from which other questions will arise. Sometimes it helps to tell members what to look for in the passage before it is read.

Preparation required:

a.   Every member will need a Bible and a sheet of paper and a pencil.

b.   The leader will need to prepare thoughtful questions.

c.   He will need to know how to guide a discussion.

d.   There should be **some way of listing findings** so that the results of the study are seen in their entirety.

An example of how to use this method.

- I Peter 3:1-13: "Peter's instructions to Married Christians."

    i. How is a Christian wife to witness for Christ to her uninterested husband?

    ii. What effect do you think a Christian wife preaching at her husband would have?

    iii. What importance should a woman place on her outward appearance?

    iv. Which is more important to a happy marriage — a pretty wife — or a gentle one?

    v. What is Peter's advice to us — whether married or not — in our attitudes to one another?

    vi. Are there any other methods a Christian wife could use to help win her husband to Christ?

19   RELATIONAL BIBLE STUDY*

i. FORGIVENESS MEANS THE NEW LIFE!

by Douglas Parker

"Thus I journeyed to Damascus with the authority and commission of the chief priests. At midday, O king, I saw on the way a light from heaven, brighter than the sun, shining round me and those who journeyed with me. And when we had all fallen to the ground, I heard a voice saying to me in the Hebrew language, 'Saul, Saul, why do you persecute me? It hurts you to kick against goads.' And I said, 'Who are you, Lord?' And the Lord said, 'I am Jesus whom you are persecuting. But rise and stand upon your feet; for I have apeared to you for this purpose, to appoint you to serve and bear witness to the things in which you have seen me and to those in which I will appear to you, delivering you from the people and from the Gentiles — to whom I send you to open their eyes, that they may turn from darkness to light and from the power of Satan to God, that they may receive forgiveness of sins and a place among those who are sanctified by faith in me."

—Acts: 26:12-18 R.S.V.

Think about Jesus before Paul, offering a break with the past but also an unknown future.

(1) Forgiveness means breaking with the past — does the prospect of that (circle one)
   (a) turn you off
   (b) make little difference
   (c) fill you with apprehension
   (d) sound scary
   (e) fill you with anticipation
   (f) makes you want to do something now.

(2) Forgiveness means putting the past behind you as Christ does — what gifts have you to share with others about your new life? Write down two of them.
   (a) ....
   (b) ....

(3) Write a letter to a person about an experience of Christian forgiveness that brought you newness of life. Take some time over this for someone has reached out to you and is counting on your letter.

(4) Share your letter with your group.

* See Chapter 3, p. 54, for an explanation of this method.

ii. FORGIVENESS MEANS FREEDOM
by Douglas Parker

They went each to his own house, but Jesus went to the Mount of Olives. Early in the morning he came again to the temple; all the people came to him, and he sat down and taught them. The scribes and the Pharisees brought a woman who had been caught in adultry, and placing her in the midst they said to him, "Teacher, this woman has been caught in the act of adultery. Now in the law Moses commanded us to stone such. What do you say about her?" This they said to test him, that they might have some charge to bring against him. Jesus bent down and wrote with his finger on the ground. As they continued to ask him, he stood up and said to them, "Let him who is without sin among you be the first to throw a stone at her." And once more he bent down and wrote with his finger on the ground. But when they heard it, they went away, one by one, beginning with the eldest, and Jesus was left alone with the woman standing before him. Jesus looked up and said to her, "Woman where are they. Has no one condemned you?" She said, "No one Lord." and Jesus said, "Neither do I condemn you; go, and do not sin again."

—John 7:53-8:11 R.S.V.

For your application:

1. Do I find it (a) easy,
   (b) hard
   (c) somewhere in between
   to accept the re-creating of life which forgiveness brings?

2. If you take the words "neither do I condemn you; go and do not sin again" seriously for you, what changes will you make in your life?

3. For me, forgiveness is...........................

iii. FORGIVENESS MEANS LOVING

by Douglas Parker

15. *When they finished breakfast, Jesus said to Simon Peter, "Simon, son of John, do you love me more than these?" He said to him, "Yes, Lord; you know that I love you." He said to him, "Feed my lambs."*
16. *A second time he said to him, "Simon, son of John, do you love me?" He said to him, "Yes, Lord; you know I love you." He said to him, "Tend my sheep."*
17. *He said to him a third time, "Simon, son of John, do you love me?" Peter was grieved because he said to him the third time, "Do you love me?" And he said to him, "Lord, you know everything; you know that I love you." Jesus said to him, "Feed my sheep."*

—John: 21:15-17. R.S.V.

For your application:

(1) Read over the Scripture passage, pausing after each sentence to let the meaning of the words sink in. (This incident happened after the resurrection of Jesus, before his ascension . . . in the period that Jesus was preparing his disciples for their mission.)

(2) Underline the words of Jesus to Peter, **Do you love me?** then close your eyes and think deeply on this question in relation to your own life. If Jesus should come to you today and ask this question of you, what would you say in all honesty?
Now write your answer............................

(3) Then, go a step further and ask yourself the question: 'What do the words "Feed my sheep" mean for me?' Or to put it simply. What is the task that God is calling me to do for Him in the world?
Some of you already know. Others have a sneaking suspicion. And some of you really do not know — and this is fine. Be honest.
Now write your answer ....

(4) What changes has loving Jesus made in you? . . .

(5) As a forgiven person, given a new life, what have you to communicate about God's forgiveness to your world?

(6) What means/ways have you at your disposal to spread love and help people experience forgiveness?

iv. **HOW ARE WE MADE OVER?**
   Scriptural Content: Acts 8:26-40

(From *Find Your Self in the Bible* by Karl A. Olsson, Augsburg, Minn., 1974. Used by permission. A book every small group leader should have.)

The story of the encounter of Philip and the Ethiopian eunuch on the road from Jerusalem to Gaza illustrates for us the problem of the transmission of the gospel: how do you make disciples? Or, put another way, how are people freed to become new in Christ and what role do we play in that *becoming?*

It is clear from our story that there is not *one* way to make disciples. But the story does suggest guidelines. Perhaps a simple listing of them will help:

1. God's redemptive action in Jesus is assumed.
2. So is the desire of the Holy Spirit to transmit the good news of redemption.
3. The means chosen by the Spirit is a chapter from Isaiah — the well known passage about the Suffering Servant from Isaiah 53. This is what the Ethiopian financier sits reading in his comfortable chariot.
4. But he needs an interpreter, someone who can explain the meaning of Isaiah 53 and also the meaning of Jesus.
5. The text tells us that "an angel of the Lord" sent Philip to the Ethiopian. Philip explains the relation of it to the gospel.
6. The effect on the Ethiopian is faith and freedom and immediate baptism and joy.

Application
In reviewing the history of the Christian enterprise, it becomes clear that our way of making disciples has included all of these steps. We have made sure that the Scriptures are made available to people in a reliable text. We have provided textual criticism, theological interpretation, preaching skills — all the work of our hundreds of well-equipped, brilliantly staffed theological schools. Beyond that we have called and trained witnesses, and we have sent them forth to win and to baptize Christian disciples. We have proclaimed our faith in the work of the Holy Spirit, and we have encouraged our converts to be free and joyful.

But if this is so, why is it that so few people seem to be "new" and to experience that "wow!" of joy which is the gift of the Holy Spirit?

106

There is certainly no problem with our explanation of the biblical word. It is, without doubt, textually correct and doctrinally sound. Do we not spend millions making sure that our ministers and missionaries are well trained and emotionally healthy?

What then is the difficulty? Could it be the explainer? Could it be that the explainer of the word which promises to give people newness of life has not himself experienced it? In the early months of 1738 when John Wesley came home after two years as an Anglican missionary in Georgia, he said, "I went to America to convert the heathen, but I found that I myself had not been converted to God." It was only after his heart had been "strangely warmed" in Aldersgate Street, May 24, 1738, that he could write, "I felt I did trust in Christ, Christ alone, for salvation; and an assurance that he had taken away *my* sins, even *mine,* and saved *me* from the law of sin and death."

The emphasis is upon *me, my,* and *mine.* To make disciples is to be personal and relational. Philip climbed into the Ethiopian's chariot, and although we do not know what he said in detail, we may be sure that he talked about the significance of Jesus and his death for him (Philip).

As I have indicated elsewhere in this book, I was myself an explainer and interpreter of the gospel and, I believe, a relatively sincere one. But I was not very personal or relational; I seem not to have conveyed clearly that I needed Jesus to make me human and personal and to help me build relationships with others. Hence I did not understand what it meant to cry "hallelujah!" At least not very loud. And I didn't set many people free.

Questions for fours

1. What one person has been the best explainer of the gospel to me and what in his or her explanation was most effective?
2. In explaining the gospel to others what one thing do I need to share which may serve to free them up and to become new beings in Christ?

Alternate question

After his re-birth or as part of it, the Ethiopian was baptized. Baptism is death and resurrection with our Lord. To what old thing do I need to die, and to what new thing do I need to be committed in the power of the Spirit?

20 ROLE PLAYING IN BIBLE STUDY

If one of the purposes of Bible study is to involve the group member in a personal way in the material being considered, then more-than-verbal methods may well be considered. The role play is a useful way of presenting a Bible passage for group study. With thought for preparation and presentation helpful insights into the passage can be given.

This can give the group member an insight into the other person's role. By adopting a different role from that in one's own personal life the role player gets on the inside of another person. It is of real value to put one's self into another's shoes. This helps the group members as they too react to the situation as presented in the role play and their feelings which are responding to the situation as it is presented. Another value can be the new light which is shed on the situation. The role play can be used in two main ways. One is directly concerned for the Bible passage. The other is concerned with personal attitudes and ideas about the Bible passage.

Remember it is important to let people talk about how they felt in their roles and to ensure that they de-role. It is important for the group members to enter as completely as possible into the discussion and share their learnings and insights gained through the role play.

Here, for **example,** is a **more than verbal approach** to the familiar **story of the prodigal son** (Luke 15:11-24).

After the story has been read, the class forms into **circles of not more than twelve, clasping hands** and crowding together so that shoulders touch. **One member absents himself** from the group and **becomes the prodigal son approaching a group** of friends and asking their help. The circle is instructed not to let the suppliant in but to **reject him** in a direct and forthright fashion, using whatever actions seem appropriate. We have found it best to use non-verbal communication of rejection. Verbal has often been too traumatic. The prodigal son **attempts to force his way through** the circle but is held out by force. He then **turns away and leaves.**

The prodigal son makes a second attempt at getting into the group. This time the **group welcomes him warmly**, **indicating** both verbally and non-verbally (with touch or embrace) that **he is wanted.**

After each member who cares to has **had the experience,** both of rejection and acceptance, **the group discusses the kinds of feelings they experienced** both **as supplicant** and **as a group member.**

The possibilities for using this kind of approach for deeper involvement in biblical stories are almost limitless. Variety, both for dialogue and for action, is virtually inexhaustible.

Other suitable stories with which this method could be used are:—

Good Samaritan
Zacchaeus
Mary and Martha
Prostitute — Jesus
    Pharisees
Unforgiving Servant
Workers in Vineyard
Mark — Paul
    Barnabas

Bartimaeus
Paul's Experiences
Philemon
Garden of Gethsemane
Woman Anointing Jesus
Pharisee and Publican in
    Temple
Woman Touching Jesus' Robe
Woman at Well
Mother Bringing Children to
    Jesus

21   SCRIPTURE ANALYSIS STUDY

(This method was used in nurture groups following evangelistic crusades conducted by Billy Graham or his team.)

Individual work

— This section is best completed prior to the group meeting.
— If it is completed by each individual during the group meeting a period of silence is maintained.
— The subject covered by the scripture passage is generally given along with the passage.
— The leader should be sure that those who are new to the method clearly understand what is expected.

The following questions are applied to the selected passage:—

A.   Discovery

   1. **What does the passage say?**
      (Write the passage in your own words. Avoid copying other translations. Try to be complete, but not "wordy". Keep the summary to an average of 6-8 words or less per verse. Ask yourself "How would this read in the newspaper?")

B.   Understanding

   2. **What don't I understand?**
      (Be honest. Is there really something you don't understand? If so, state clearly.)

   3. **Key verse**
      (a) **What is the Key Verse in this passage?**
          (Carefully read the passage several times. Select the verse which sums up the entire passage.)
      (b) **Why is this the Key Verse?**

C.   Application

   4. (a) **What impresses ME most?**
          (The passage in its entirety, a portion, or a single verse may challenge you to some area of personal obedience or action. Write this out **using the personal pronoun "I".**)

(b) **Where do I come short in this?**
(State specifically where you fail in the above challenge. **Use personal pronoun "I".**

(c) **What do I intend to do about it, with God's help?**
Try to write a specific plan that **you** will follow to apply the above challenge **to your own** life.

GROUP DISCUSSION

A. Discovery
— Each member shares his or her paraphrase of the passage.
— The leader may help further understanding of the meaning and relationship to other truths by dividing the passage from the Bible into sections, if possible, and preparing good thought-provoking questions based on the passage.

B. Understanding
— Each member shares what he does not understand about the passage.
— The leader asks if anyone has found anything from another part of the Bible that will help in understanding this passage.
(Thus each will be able to take part at every stage of the discussion by drawing on what he has previously prepared, as well as on thoughts which come to him at the time.)
— Each shares his Key Verse with reasons for selecting the verse.

C. Application
— The aim of this segment is to stimulate each member to transfer the truths learned from his head to his heart and out into his life.
— Individual written applications are shared around the group.
— The leader may suggest that each makes a note of the others' applications so that each can pray specifically for the others during the week and thus fulfil Galatians 6:2, "Bear one another's burdens . . ."
— The group is encouraged to apply one truth at a time.

SUGGESTED TOPICS AND SCRIPTURE PASSAGES

Subject

First Ten Weeks:
1. Looking to Jesus
2. Love
3. The Word of God
4. Praying to God
5. Following Jesus Christ
6. Telling about Jesus Christ
7. Abiding in Christ
8. Faith in God
9. Forgiveness of Sins
10. God's Protection and Guidance

Second Ten Weeks:
11. Doing Good Works
12. The Tongue
13. Temptation
14. Relationships of Work
15. Family Relationships
16. Jesus Christ, the Son of God
17. The Death of Christ
18. The Lord's Supper
19. The Resurrection of the Dead
20. Truth

Passage

Hebrews 12:1-4
I Corinthians 13:1-8
2 Timothy 3:10-4:8
Matthew 6:5-15 & 7:7-11
Mark 8:27-38
Acts 8:26-40
John 15:1-11
Hebrews 11:1-16
1 John 1:5-2:2
John 10:7 and 27-30

Titus 2:11-3:8
James 3
Matthew 4:1-20
Colossians 3:22-4:1
Ephesians 5:21-6:4
Colossians 1:13-29
Romans 5:1-11
1 Corinthians 11:23-32
1 Corinthians 15:35-58
John 8:21-38

22   BIBLE ROLE PLAY

(Adapted from Robert C. Leslie's book, *Sharing Groups in the Church,* pages 31-44).

The Bible is a document of timeless experiences about which everyone knows something in his own life. By talking about his personal experiences, each individual speaks as an expert about the life that he knows best.

Introduction

Read the Scripture reference out loud using different voices for different characters where applicable, as well as a narrator for continuity, and using modern translations freely.

Thus, even before the study begins a number of the group members are involved actively in the procedure.

Small groups

1. **Discuss the associations stirred up in your mind by the passage of Scripture.** You are an expert on what associations come to your mind. **Share** these associations **in as personal a way as you can** with the study group. (If the group is more than twelve, divide into **groups of about six.)**
    The leader can help set a contemporary note by sharing an association of present-day life and encourage personal associations by group members to the story.

2. **In small groups discuss the following question** "What do you think this story is really about in terms of **relationships between people?"**
    As the small groups struggle with this question, they begin to sense the **contemporary relevance of the Bible.** Only at this point is biblical interpretation introduced. There obviously is a place for informed understanding about biblical research. The point is, however, that the Bible so often gives examples of **life experiences that are typical of any age** so that specific contexts are less important than the central message.

3. **In the same small groups discuss your reaction to . . .** (Here the leader introduces **an aspect** of the story which **might have been overlooked,** and in so doing he may raise a major theological question: This can lead easily into the next issue.)

Plenary

Discuss together in the **large group** with the leader what it means to . . . (Here, the **main theme** of the story can be discussed).

Robert Leslie gives **two examples** of the method:—

"**The first** based upon the story of Joseph and his brothers in Genesis 37:2-8, 12, 28 illustrates steps (4) and (5) well. Under (4) he chooses Genesis 45:5 ("God sent me before you to preserve life") and follows this up in (5) by asking the large group to discuss "what it means to live a life directed by God."

"**The second** focuses upon the story of Zacchaeus in Luke 19:1-9. Under (3) he asks, Have you ever been 'up a tree' like Zacchaeus? When have you felt cut off? The plenary discussion (4) follows naturally: When you felt cut off, what helped?

"This discussion leads easily into a consideration of how Jesus went about reaching Zacchaeus and of the meaning of an invitation to have a meal at home."

He then suggests an additional item of discussion—

"In the same group of six, discuss the meaning of Luke 19:9 ("And Jesus said to him, 'Today salvation has come to this house, since he also is a son of Abraham' ").

After the small groups have talked together about the meaning of "salvation", the leader can interpret salvation as a new kind of relatedness, a relationship that includes both the man-to-man (i.e. Zacchaeus restored to his Jewish community from which he had been alienated) and the man-to-God (wrong relationships made right) dimensions."

23   SILENT SHARING METHOD

This method is very simple and may be used with all age groups. It is also **a good means of introducing young people to Bible Study for the first time.**

Method of approach:

a. Give instructions to the group before indicating the passage they are to read.

b. Tell the group that they are to look for a verse which either **"Means most to me in this particular passage"** OR **"Sheds new light on the Christian life"** OR **"Is God's message to me at this moment."**

c. Inform them that this step is done individually and in silence.

d. Indicate that **they will be asked to share their answers** when they have finished reading.

e. Now give the Bible reference to be studied.

f. Leader should read also and should be prepared to share first.

g. Others in the group share also. Significant answers may be recorded on a chalkboard or chartpaper.

h. If some share the same verse, they may have different reasons for choosing it.

Preparation required:

i. Every person needs a Bible.

ii. Choose the passage carefully according to the needs of the group.

iii. Have a chalkboard or chart paper on which findings can be recorded.
    Some suggested Scripture passages:

Romans 12:9-21.	Ephesians 4:1-16.
Psalm 139:1-10.	1 Cor. 13:1-13.
John 15:1-14.	Col. 3:12-17.

24   THE SIX C's

Each member will need their own copy of the Bible, pencil and paper. The group will need an hour for this study and time should be allocated to each section before commencement. It is suggested that the time be divided evenly into the six parts.

1. **Choose** a Bible passage for study.

2. **Call** upon God for the guidance of His Holy Spirit. Praying may be done silently and individually or as group prayer.

3. **Characterize** the event. Picture the scene. Try to understand the people. What sort of people are they? Perhaps individuals can share books they have read or pictures seen which may throw new light on the event or scene.

4. **Consider** what the passage is really saying. What does it mean? Why is it included in the Bible? Has it a meaning for today?

5. **Comment** on three special points which are significant. Which are the most important?

6. **Concerns for the church.** In considering the above points, discuss: (a) Their relevance to the outreach of the church and parish, (b) Do they touch the life of the parish, and if so, how? (c) If not, how may the truth be applied?

25 SWEDISH SYMBOL SHARING METHOD

This part throws new light on to my understanding or shows me something I never realised before.

This challenges me in some way or pricks my conscience.

I do not understand this word, phrase or verse or I do not agree with it.

This is a very effective method **for a group not used to Bible study.** The passage chosen is read either aloud by the leader, using expression, or by the group as a whole so that they are all involved right from the beginning.

Individual study of the text follows for ten minutes, each person using the three symbols. Either explain the meaning of the symbols to the group before the study OR give each member a card or sheet of paper with the symbols and their explanation printed thereon. The **group comes together** to share their markings under each symbol at a time. These should be recorded on a chalk board or substitute.

General discussion may follow.

Most suited for: Parables of Jesus.
Sections from the Epistles.

Preparation required:

a. Find a suitable passage. If members are a bit hesitant about marking their Bibles, provide the passage on a separate sheet of paper.

b. If using cards to introduce the symbols, have sufficient for every member.

c. Have a **chalkboard or substitute for the summary** at the end.

d. Have Concordances, Dictionaries, and Commentaries available, if needed, to clarify any points which may arise from the question marks.

e. The leader does the study as well, and usually is prepared to share his/her reactions first.

f. If many members have the same phrases and verses marked it is wise to get them to share their reasons for marking them.

Examples of passages which could be used for this method.

> Ephesians 2:13-20.
> Matthew 20:1-16.
> Luke 7:36-50.

WORKSHEET

SYMBOL	VERSE	COMMENT
THIS THROWS NEW LIGHT ON TO MY UNDERSTANDING OR — SHOWS ME SOMETHING I NEVER REALISED BEFORE.		
THIS CHALLENGES ME IN SOME WAY OR — PRICKS MY CONSCIENCE.		
I DO NOT UNDERSTAND THIS WORD, PHRASE OR VERSE. OR — I DO NOT AGREE WITH IT.		

26   TEN QUESTIONS

This method is particularly useful in a direct teaching situation when the leader and group are working through a book of the Bible in a systematic way. It is also a helpful way for those who are relatively new to Bible study.

Members divide into small groups of 4 and are given a Bible passage to study. From that passage they choose 10 question which they would either like clarified, answered, or have the opportunity to discuss.

After 15 minutes, the group report to the leader their questions and they are written up on a board or flip chart where all may see.

The remainder of the time may be given to the leader to

(a) lead the discussion of the large group till they find satisfactory answers to their questions.
(b) move through the passage and as a teacher to impart more information on the problem questions, as well as explaining background, words, etc.
(c) give to each group a research task. This would require commentaries, concordances etc. to be provided and for the leader to give guidance if needed and requested. The findings should be fed back to the large assembled group.

27 BIBLICAL SIMULATIONS

When we speak of simulation, we mean any reenactment of an event in which there is an attempt to portray accurately some selected elements of that event. Currently simulation has taken on the highly positive meaning of reenacting an event so as to bring certain features of that event directly and powerfully before us. Simulation has often proven to be more effective in putting us into a situation than description, lecture, movie, discussion, or other methods of presentation where participants talk about an event rather than live in it.

Simulation begins by portraying a situation accurately in order that whatever truth is there may be perceived and further explored. Yet simulations may be dramatic.

What is a Biblical simulation?

A biblical simulation is the **reenactment** of some particular biblical event in an attempt to portray accurately some selected features of that event. In brief, the purpose is to bring a biblical event into a present lived moment.

Our definition suggests that a simulation is **an accurate portrayal.** We want to be accurate in portraying the attitudes and points of view represented in a biblical account. Far more important is the appreciation of the convictions of the persons being portrayed.

Finally, our definition of biblical simulation focuses upon the **selected elements** of an event.

Rules should be suggested for each simulation that will allow for maximum exploration of the background of the event and for contact between various opinions. The rules and procedure are pre-established, so that everyone knows what is happening and when the simulation is concluded. Clarity of procedure will allow everyone to participate more fully in the actual discussion.

Again it is important to remember that once the situation is established, it may go where it will. Whichever direction the simulation goes, it will throw new light on the passages being studied. A living dialogue between real points of view will be much more instructive than merely mimicking the sequence as recorded.

Why then use biblical simulations? What is their purpose? Far beyond curiosity and novelty their purpose is to allow scriptural events to be lived deeply, imaginatively, and intensely. They are designed to combine playfulness with discipline, imagination with study, not so much because such an approach is new, but rather because the Holy Spirit Himself exhibits these qualities throughout the Bible. Their purpose is to encourage within us a trust that can tolerate conflict and a hope that finds God's kingdom breaking in among us. Their purpose is to let the past be present in order that the future may be ours. When in the past people have been able to identify closely with the Scripture, there has been a renewal of faith. Our hope for renewal again lies in a deeper understanding of the meaning and power of the biblical message.

For further information and a number of actual simulations of biblical stories you should refer to one of the most comprehensive books on the subject. The book is Donald Miller et al: *Using Biblical Simulations* (Judson Press, Valley Forge, 1973).

28 CREATIVE EXPRESSION

Most of the Bible studies in this book have been limited to verbal or written expression. For those a little more adventurous, creative expression of what you interpret the Bible to be saying can be a very "freeing" and enriching experience.

We need also to remember that some people have a real difficulty reading and expressing themselves verbally. The exploration of other ways of interpretation is an encouragement to them as they feel their contribution is accepted, and they in turn feel themselves accepted and a worthwhile member of the group.

Another advantage of creative expression is that one has to think more deeply about a passage to express it in this way. This work may be done as "homework" between meetings to allow for more thought, concentration and time. However, some extremely good work can be, and is, done quite quickly. Some people are stimulated by being able to express themselves in a free, non-critical atmosphere.

Some ideas only (Let the Holy Spirit kindle your imagination!)

1. **Take a word,** "salvation", for example, and express its meaning by a montage (pictures and words cut from magazines and posted on paper). This allows for a diversity of "sub-headings" which together give a better picture of the totality of the word. Members may like to discuss one another's contribution before beginning the study for the day — which may be on that topic **or** it may be an expression of what has been previously discussed.

2. **Writing a poem or prayer**
Two alternatives need to be given if possible so that at least one method is always on any one member's level of achievement. Many have hidden gifts for writing poems and some creative writing has been done when this opportunity was given. Some equally creative and inspiring prayers have resulted from others.

3. **Drama**

Try some spontaneous "acting out" of a story; perhaps you could give it a modern setting or take one facet of an incident reported in the Bible. For example, if the group is discussing the healing of the blind man, take it in turns blindfolding one's partner and leading them around the house. Discuss how it felt to be blind — what did it feel like to see? etc.

4. **Painting or drawing**

Take a theme like "I am the Light of the World" John 8:12 and illustrate using paints or craypas or textas.

5. **Write a play or a musical drama**

This may be done as a group effort or by two people working on it together.

6. **Other ideas**

Making a mobile, clay modelling, abstract modelling from bits and pieces, writing a song or finding a song that expresses the theme of a passage.

Create a collage using scrap materials — cloth, paper, foil, ribbons, laces, herbs, seeds (e.g. mustard seed, lentils, sunflower and pumpkin [these are edible], etc.) The collage can be abstract and symbolic (expressing feelings, concepts) or realist in style (depicting incidents).

Created by a group on a large scale and combined with montage, painting or weaving can be used to decorate a room to create an atmosphere of worship, or express joy, etc.

If working systematically through a book of the Bible, creative expression, together with a variety of other Bible study methods, will give a freshness of approach and a new vitality to the group. It is important to remember that we don't have to be artists to paint. What is wanted is the expression of that person's thoughts — if masterpieces are expected, the whole purpose of freedom of expression is defeated.

Encouragement needs to be given to members to "try". Most will hesitate, especially the first few times, but it won't be long before many talents will be appearing which may have been either dormant or undiscovered.

5 Prayer in Small Groups

The experience of the Church has been that there is no real progress in true Christianity without prayer. Periods of spiritual power in the Church have been preceded by and sustained by, great prayer. No limit can be put to its power. Yet most of us in the Church will confess that too often we have busied ourselves with countless matters other than prayer. More often than not we trust in our animal energy and activity rather than in the Holy Spirit. I suspect sometimes that we are overdependent on plans and policy to the neglect of prayer.

Dietrich Bonhoeffer writes:

"We are separated from one another by an unbridgeable gulf of otherness and strangeness which resists all our attempts to overcome it by means of natural association or emotional or spiritual union, for there are no direct relationships, not even between soul and soul. Christ stands between us, and we can only get into touch with our neighbours through him. That is why intercession is the most promising way to reach our neighbours, and corporate prayer, offered in the name of Christ, the purest form of fellowship."[1]

In small groups people are rediscovering the power released through prayer. In small face to face group situations, people are exploring together the meaning and purpose of prayer. They are taking God's promises seriously. Barren stereotyped procedures which have straightjacketed much of our past small group prayer are being discarded and new and exciting skills in communicating with God are being developed. The power of the Holy Spirit, in His role as the divine enabler in prayer, is being experienced anew.

The new interest in prayer

In 1968 a significant meeting of Anglican Bishops in Lambeth made the statement, "The primary task of the Church is to glorify God by leading all mankind into life in Christ and this always involves a continuous advance in the practice of prayer in the Spirit. The Bishops attending this Conference therefore call upon the clergy and laity of the whole Anglican Communion to join with them in the determination in humble and penitent dependence upon God, to deepen and strengthen their life of prayer, remembering always that our Lord's periods of withdrawal for prayer were a prelude and preparation of his further service in the world that the Father might be glorified.

"To this end, the Church should search to discover those forms of spirituality and methods of prayer, both corporate and personal, which meet the needs of men and women today . . . The Church should pay more attention to the development of that capacity for silent prayer which exists in all her members and should encourage corporate and personal waiting upon God."

This call to prayer was answered by many with renewed attention to their own prayer life and by the formation of prayer cells. The large Anglican Prayer Fellowship in the U.S.A. through the thousands of small prayer groups associated with it, its Schools of Prayer and numerous resources, along with many other innovations in the churches of the Anglican tradition, has done much to fulfil the challenge of that Lambeth call to prayer.

One of the signs of renewed interest in prayer is from young people. Youth are now showing an increasing interest in the mystical aspects of life. Thousands of young people are joining groups for yoga, transcendental meditation, and other disciplines from eastern religions.

In the Christian church many new and encouraging prayer movements are springing up involving both old and young.

The Taize Community in France is an ecumenical community of over 80 headed up by a Lutheran priest, Brother Roger. It has opened its doors for any visitors to share its prayer disciplines and find a refuge for contemplation. Young people come in ever increasing numbers from all over the world. A Youth Council was formed after it was decided that contact with young people should be an ongoing feature of life at the community. After four years preparation by an international team of young people the opening took place in August 1974. Forty thousand people from more than a hundred nations arrived to share in the opening and the weekend of contemplation. Thousands come weekly and the only reason the community leaders can give is "Because we pray". Many small cell groups form as a result of attendance, with three marked ingredients which constitute healthy group life — prayer, sharing of material possessions and service outside the group.

Easter 1976 marked a new break-through. Weekends of preparation were followed by people going by two's into communities and parishes of different countries to search together for deeper levels of Christian understanding and meditative life-style.

A few years ago, while in Switzerland, I interviewed a Salvation Army Captain from Sweden who reported on the 10,000 prayer cells involving youth and adults which have sprung up in Stockholm.

In Australia we cannot give reports like that from Sweden, but there are clear signs of this work of the Spirit amongst Protestants and Catholics. The healing ministry, such as the Order of St. Luke the Physician, is drawing many together in small groups for prayer. The charismatic movement has helped many come alive to the power of personal and corporate prayer.

Both within and outside the church structures, small groups gather for prayer. Sometimes it may be just two or three concerned people meeting spontaneously in an informal manner. In some situations there are clusters of groups. Many prayer cells meet across denominational boundaries. All this is evidence of the Spirit's work in drawing people together to praise their God and pray with new concern.

However, I find that many people really want to pray but don't know how. Most are very limited in their prayer experience. For many, the extent of their learning in prayer has been listening to public prayers, or the reciting by rote of prayers they learnt in their childhood.

Jesus responded to the expressed need of His disciples — "Lord, teach us to pray" by guiding them in **how** to pray as well as **what** to pray. It would seem that many people are asking the same questions today. The response to the prayer workshops I have conducted has shown that people are longing to be taught how to pray and what to pray for. I can never recall receiving any instruction in the art of prayer from any person who ministered to me in a parish situation. Exhortations to prayer there were, but nothing I can recollect on how to make prayer come alive.

In small groups we have an ideal situation to provide help for people in personal and corporate prayer.

One of the finest resources I have come across for this two-fold task has been published by the Upper Room, Nashville, Tennessee, *The Workbook of Living Prayer,* by Maxie Dunnam. It is a practical guide arranged in six major divisions each containing seven sections to help develop personal prayer, one for each day of the week. It is also designed to allow for a group venture with suggestions to facilitate sharing at a weekly meeting.

In the next two chapters I have given a variety of methods to enable group prayer to become more dynamic.

Why Pray with others

There are many reasons why we should meet with others; I suggest three — because Jesus prayed with others; the early church practised it and because there are real advantages in praying together.

Christ taught us to pray individually in isolation and He did it Himself. But that was only one aspect of His prayer life. Even when He withdrew to a quiet place this was not necessarily for solitary prayer. "As He was praying alone the disciples were with Him" (Luke 9:18). Peter, James and John were with Him on the high mountain (Luke 9:28) and accompanied Him into the Garden of Gethsemane. To record His prayer in Mark 14:33 they must have overheard it. The Lord also prayed habitually with the apostles. If we are to be His disciples, to "learn" from Him, we must pray alone and we must pray with others.

From the very beginning the apostolic church was a community at prayer. It was upon a company at prayer that the Holy Spirit was poured out on the Day of Pentecost (Acts 1:14). The first converts "joined with the other believers in regular attendance at the apostles' teaching sessions and at the breaking of bread services in prayer". In the crisis of persecution the assembled Church spontaneously resorted to prayer (Acts 4:23-31). When Peter was imprisoned and threatened with execution "many were gathered for a prayer meeting" in the house of Mary, mother of John Mark (Acts 12:12). Barnabas and Paul were dedicated for their special task following a time of prayer and fasting by a small group of five church leaders in Antioch (Acts 13:1-3).

There are some real advantages in praying together. Jesus was insistent that we find solitude and be alone with God. But He also said that the mind and will of God can come to us more clearly when we pray with others.

> *"If two of you agree on earth about anything they ask, it will be done for them by my Father in Heaven. For where two or three are gathered in my name, there am I in the midst of them." (Matt 18:19-20).*

When we pray alone it is difficult to sift our selfish desires from our real needs and our own will from God's intentions. So when we pray with another as a group, we have the advantage of testing our assessment of God's will against the group's insights.

From that same passage in Matthew we deduce the greatest advantage of praying together — the promised presence of Christ in the midst of that fellowship. All through the ages when Christians have assembled for prayer with a common purpose and a deep sense of unity they have been aware of the unseen Presence and have encountered the living Lord.

> "There is also a deeper joy in praying together, an added vitality, a plus difficult to define. It is rather like the difference between eating your meal alone and sharing in a party feast. Eating together is not the same as eating in solitude; the something more is the company, the fellowship. So it is with prayer."[2]

In his latest book, *The Exciting Church Where People Really Pray* (Word), Charlie Shedd gives some convincing and heartwarming evidence of the advantages of praying with others. The second section of the book is headed, "Where the People Pray — These Good things Happen". In eight short chapters he lists and illustrates these "Good Things": "They Care for Each Other; Lives will be Changed; They Attract New Members; There Will be Social Concern; They Also Serve the Church; They Reach Out to the World; The Little Negatives Stay Little; Everyone is Able to Serve."

There are some wild (and mild) misconceptions abroad about prayer which need to be dispelled if group and personal prayer is to fulfil the purpose God intended for it.

— Living prayer is not purely a ritual — being limited to a formal practice, following a prescribed order or book of rites.

— It is not limited to a few set formulae. Inflexibility is foreign to real communication between Father and sons and daughters. Patterns to follow should be used as means not ends. Written prayers can be of great benefit but they should not dominate and restrict.

— It is not a way of manipulating God to get our own way.

— It is not purely a panic button to use only when we have our backs against the wall, nor an escape hatch to survive a crisis situation. God certainly does answer our S.O.S. calls. But, if the radio waves only carried distress signals it would be one-sided tiresome communication.

— It is not a magic wand to help us perform our own special brand of miracles. Some dear souls give the impression they would like to get into the act by performing their own miracle and in prayer invite God on to their side to make it happen! As though we were the miracle workers rather than merely the humble channels through which God in His own time and way breaks into the order of His world.

— It is not purely a therapeutic exercise. "Learn to pray so you can relax" — a short course in how to rip God off for your own ends. Of course it is therapeutic, I know of few better ways to find peace of mind — but that is a by-product. Its main purpose is to honour and revere God. Any purely selfish purpose is greatly inferior to its central function.

— It is not preaching or airing our theological knowledge to impress others.

— It is not a short Cook's tour of the world and its needs by one person while some reverent souls sit patiently at the point of departure hoping for their brother to return, soon!! Conversational prayer has helped many groups with this problem.

What prayer is   Prayer is listening. It is being still to know that God is God.

Prayer is contemplation. It is thinking about God in long periods of silence. It is deep thought and meditation with expectation.

Prayer is a fleeting thought directed to God.

Prayer is a deep unuttered desire within a human heart.

Prayer is talking to God. It is a 'child' talking to a loving Heavenly Father.

Prayer is an instantaneous cry for help.

Prayer is conversation. It is both talking and listening.

Prayer is communion. It is a meeting between two who are in love. The Eternal Source of all Agape Love reaches down to touch a human being who makes an inadequate response.

Prayer is the faltering words of a person with no faith probing for **God** of Whom he is uncertain, in a search for reality and meaning.

Prayer is a grain of faith moving a person to ask and expect miracles.

Prayer is breathing, spiritually. "It is a Christian's vital breath, the Christian's native air".

Prayer is affirming God. It is bringing delight to God — making Him glad.

Prayer is saying "I'm sorry" to God and asking for grace not to repeat our failure.

Prayer is asking forgiveness for God's sake as well as for our sake.

Prayer is bringing the big challenges and responsibilities of life to God and receiving His divine enablement.

Prayer is having faith to bring the mundane 'non-events', the routine, small things of life to God believing he cares for the insignificant 'lilies of the field', 'the birds of the air' and how much more for us.

Prayer is both asking and receiving.

Prayer is bringing to God my deep concern for those who are near to me, my family, my close circle of friends.

Prayer is acknowledging my membership in this global village and praying as specifically as I can for my brothers and sisters in this world who are unknown to me by name.

Prayer is laying before God a concern for our enemies.

Prayer is the way to inner serenity — it is the calm found in the 'eye' of the hurricane, not an escape from the turmoils of life.

Prayer is where I meet my risen Lord — where I learn to know Him and the power of His resurrection.

Prayer is a child's simplest form of communication with God.

Prayer is an art which none of the saints felt they had fully mastered.

Prayer is praying when we don't feel like talking with God because we believe He is always loving us, always listening, always wanting to bless us with His grace and love.

Prayer is a family conversing with God. It is the deepest of human fellowship.

Prayer is keeping my contribution short when praying with others to help their concentration and giving them a fair share of the conversation with our Father.

Prayer is honesty and openness with God, both when I pray in solitude and when I pray with others.

Prayer is work.

Prayer is believing the "Holy Spirit within us is actually praying for us in those agonising longings which never find words".

Prayer is where our hope in confirmed, our faith strengthened, our love enriched, our authenticity increased, and a depth and sensitivity given to life which can be found nowhere else.

Some foundations for prayer

At the Memorial Day Drive Presbyterian Church in Houston, Texas, the Rev. Charlie Shedd enabled the congregation to come alive as a "praying church". Five hundred people prayed by a special covenant. To help them understand what they are doing and have a sound theological platform from which to pray certain basic precepts were taught the members. In his book *How to Develop a Praying Church*, Charlie Shedd gives a brief summary of each precept.

"Prayer is for discovering God's will. We do not pray in order that we might get what we want. Prayer is for finding out what God wants from us. We pray in order that we might become instruments for His glory.

"The first move of prayer is God's move. We do not initiate the divine-human encounter. Prayer is not the business of finding God. It is rather a matter of being found by the God who made man for himself.

"Pray in your own way! There are twelve gates into the holy city and a thousand different doors to prayer. When we pray we are entering a vast expanse of truth which leaves room for much experiment and many approaches.

"Intercession is not optional! We are to pray for others because Jesus said we should. Scripture is replete with instructions that those who take part in the church that is striving to be God's church will be praying for their fellow members."

In this book it is not my purpose to give a treatise on the theology of prayer. There are others far better qualified from their knowledge and personal experience who have dealt adequately with the underlying doctrines of this theme. I always find it a rewarding exercise to search out this theme, or to read the prayers in the Bible, with the help of a concordance or a Topical Bible.

A small group which hopes to grow in its prayer life must have a good grasp of Biblical teaching to make a firm base for their prayers. The purpose, potential, and possibilities of the Christian's prayers are arrived at by studying God's revealed word on the matter. The many books on the subject only supplement this data.

The perfect pattern for prayer

In answer to His disciples' request, Jesus gave to them and to us, what has become known as The Lord's Prayer. The pattern it sets out is very simple, but very comprehensive. It is at one and the same time a prayer to use by itself and a pattern for all prayer. Many small groups are finding an enriching experience as they study the prayer at depth.

Some using a resource such as *The Plain Man Looks at The Lord's Prayer* by William Barclay have taken a section at a time to expand their understanding of prayer. Others have benefited from paraphrasing the prayer individually or as a group. The pattern which the prayer follows has been studied by some groups which then follow this outline for private and group prayer experiences over a period to give direction to their own prayer. Maxie Dunnam's *Workbook of Living Prayer* suggests two seven-day segments working through The Lord's Prayer and then using the pattern as a base for further growth.

In *The Plain Man Looks at the Lord's Prayer,* Barclay at the beginning of the second chapter, looks at the general pattern of the prayer before giving a detailed study.

"We cannot fail to see that the prayer begins by giving God His own and His proper place. The first three petitions of the prayer are for the hallowing of God's name, the coming of God's Kingdom, and the doing of God's will. It is only then that we turn to our own needs and our own requests. The great fault of prayer is that it can so easily become self-centred and self-seeking.

"It begins by putting, not us, but God in the centre of the picture.

"The second part of the prayer is the most comprehensive prayer that men were ever taught to pray. Let us set down its three petitions:

Give us this day our daily bread.

Forgive us our debts, as we forgive our debtors.

Lead us not into temptation, but deliver us from evil.

"These three short petitions take life, past present and future, and lay it before God. Food for the present, forgiveness for the past, help for the future — all of life is brought into the presence of God.

"But these three petitions do even more than that. When we pray the first of them, the prayer for daily bread, we think of **God the Father**, the Creator and Sustainer of all life. When we pray the second of them, the prayer for our forgiveness, we think of **God the Son,** the Saviour and Redeemer of all mankind and of us. When we pray the third of them, the prayer for future help to live without sin, we think of **God the Holy Spirit,** the Guide, the Helper and the Protector of all life. These three petitions bring us face to face with Father, Son and Holy Spirit. Within their narrow compass, and with their astonishing economy of words, these three brief petitions take the whole of life to the whole of God.

"The pattern of the Lord's Prayer must be the pattern of all prayer, for it begins by giving God His proper place, and it goes on to take life's past, present and future to God, the Father, Son, and Holy Spirit."

Helmut Thielicke in *The Prayer that Spans the World,* (another good resource book) likens the Lord's Prayer to the rainbow colours of the spectrum. "The whole light of life is captured in this rainbow of seven petitions". He gives another refreshing interpretation of this the greatest of the Christian's prayer resources. Numerous other books are on the market to assist the group in plumbing the depth of this immortal prayer.

The study of the Lord's Prayer will open up the order in which Christians have found it helpful to pray. It may help to deal with them here and make some comments which are applicable to prayer in small groups.

The forms of prayer

Adoration is the rarest of all prayers. We do not even say thank you, we simply adore. We think of the greatness of God — How incredible that He should bother to hear us at all. Dwell on the person of God, His nature, His greatness. Contemplation and meditation are lost arts which many Protestants are re-discovering with the help of writers such as the Trappist monk, Thomas Merton.

It often helps to view a scene from a mountain look-out. Stand on a cliff overlooking the sea or concentrate upon a flower. A picture of these can be used as an aid. An appropriate passage of Scripture from the Psalms, Isaiah chapters 6 and 40, or others describing Christ, His nature and purpose such as Philippians 2:5-11 or Pentecost can be meditated upon, leading to adoration.

It is unnatural for this prayer to be prayed in isolation from other forms. But it is a good discipline, even in a group, to try it occasionally.

Confession in group prayer is best undertaken in silence. Don't hurry this. Allow a time to recall past failures. Encourage the group to be specific. Bidding prayers can help: "Think of a relationship with another that you may not have taken the initiative to heal" or: "Think of words you may have spoken which have not been suitable for the occasion" or "What action spoilt your witness last week; yesterday?" Assure them of forgiveness as they have asked for forgiveness in the Name of Jesus; quote a promise such as John 1:9. Encourage the group to accept by faith, apart from feelings, what God offers to them by His grace. In silence, or audibly, let them then praise Him in general terms.

In our prayer workshops we have found it helpful to have participants write the sins they confess on a piece of paper. Then, as an act of faith, they draw a cross over what they have written and tear the slip into small pieces. A paper cup is passed around each group to receive the pieces. As it is passed around the person passing it says to the next person — "As you have confessed your sins to God, in the Name of Jesus you are forgiven". On occasions we have completed the confession and assurance of forgiveness by placing the contents of the paper cups in a large metal can and sent one person outside to burn them. The person has sometimes returned saying, "The records of our sins are completely consumed in the fire of God's love in Christ, praise be to God". The groups reply, "Praise be to God, His grace is sufficient for all our sins, blessed be His Holy name!"

The general confession (Psalm 51) particularly in a modern translation is a useful form of group confession. To paraphrase 1 John 1:9 individually can help confirm the reality of God's love and forgiveness.

Thanksgiving is the natural step to follow an experience of the certainty of forgiveness through God's grace in Jesus. Again help people to be specific. Bidding prayers can further help as people go over particular experiences of God's goodness. For example: "Reflect on persons, situations, experiences you can be genuinely grateful for at home this week". "Can you recall a time when you have been specially loved or had the opportunity to show love since last we met?" "Can you remember the gratitude you felt as you lay down to rest after a hard day's work?" Health, friends, books, fun, work, life's challenges (and a thousand others!) are all topics for thanksgiving.

Thanksgiving should also include expectations of future fulfilment as an affirmation of our faith in God's ability to answer our prayers.

It will also go beyond ourselves to thanking God for the blessings others have received in the group and beyond the group to our friends and widening out to world situations.

Petition is the next step. W. E. Sangster says "Some masters of prayer have no place for personal petition. Clement of Alexandria had none. He, and many like him, were content to leave God to give them what was good. Yet Jesus taught petition . . . and that was enough. But keep petition in a minor place. Nothing more reveals the juvenility of our prayers if we pray with persistence and passion only when we want something for ourselves."[3]

Again we should be specific. It is helpful to have each member write out a prayer of petition as a response to a meaningful Bible study segment. These can then be prayed silently or audibly around the group in turn. Each can be followed by members putting their hand on the person next to them and praying, "Lord grant . . .'s prayer". Some find it helpful to keep a confidential spiritual diary in which they record prayer responses to significant learning experiences.

Intercession, or praying for others, is selfless prayer. In it we exercise one of the most sacred aspects of the ministry to which we all are called. This is our "priestly" role. We become "bridge-builders" between people in their need and God, the source of undeserved favour. A concerned person listens for expressed needs rather than inventing his own assessment of another's needs. Again prayers need to be specific. Avoid allowing the gathering of information about others for prayer which degenerates into gossip. In a number of groups we have found it helpful to keep a prayer list. This not only prompts specific regular intercession but engenders specific thanksgiving as answers to prayer are noted from one meeting to another.

Dedication is an aspect which follows naturally after intercession. This is the "Lord here am I, send me" response to human need or "with eyes wide open to your mercy I present myself to you Lord, as the least I can do. Use me as you will". It may be incorporated in Petition but it is often appropriate to make it a separate act of prayer. Sincere dedication can be an awesome thing — Acts 4:29-31.

The place of the Bible in prayer

The Bible has an important role to play in personal and corporate prayer. One person has said it comes alive as the Word of God when read and responded to in the context of prayer.

The Bible should be the heart of the corporate life of the group. The greatest contribution the Bible makes to prayer is that is reveals to us the true nature of the Divine Person to whom we offer our prayers. Even groups which have prayer as their main aim seldom, if ever, maintain real vitality without regular and frequent references and meditation upon the Bible.

The Bible is a treasure house of written prayers from the stories of some of the greatest persons in prayer the world shall ever know. Jesus, the patriarchs, the prophets, the psalmists and the apostles all have left us an eternal heritage of prayers prayed in real life situations. Here is a sample of some of these prayer resources the Bible provides:

Prayer for preservation and protection — Numbers 10:35-36.

Prayer for a sick child — II Samuel 12.

Prayer for understanding of affliction — Samuel 21:1-12.

Prayer in national danger — II Chronicles 14:11.

Prayer as intercession — Job 42:7-10.

Prayer for preservation here and hereafter — Psalm 16.

Prayer for confession and a broken heart — Psalm 51.

Prayer for peace — Isaiah 26.

Prayer for the oppressed — Lamentations 5.

Prayer as taught by Christ — Matthew 6:1-13.

Prayer habits of Christ — Mark 1:35.

The intercessory prayer of Jesus — John 17.

The role of the Holy Spirit in prayer

The Holy Spirit is God at work in us in the here and now. He is our life. Prayer comes alive not because we have correct understanding of the theology of prayer, nor because we have developed some special techniques or because of our regular disciplined application to its pursuit, but essentially because God is in it. The Holy Spirit is the key to vital prayer life, individually or corporately.

"And in the same way — by our faith — the Holy Spirit helps us with our daily problems and in our praying. For we don't even know what we should pray for nor how to pray as we should; but the Holy Spirit prays for us with such feeling that it cannot be expressed in words. And the Father who knows all hearts knows, of course, what the Spirit is saying as he pleads for us in harmony with God's own will." (Romans 8:26-27).

Because the Holy Spirit is our special Partner who helps us make our Christian life pleasing to God we will need to have a clear grasp of who He is and what we may expect Him to do for us and in us. "I think of Him as the roving Centre of all God's activity in the world. He is the Inspirer of all Truth . . . He is the Creator of all beauty . . . He is in every work of mercy, in every good and gentle life, in every reconciliation between estranged people or groups, in every lift of the spirits of overtaxed and suffering people . . . He is God in His wildest, most ingenious, most far-flung aspects. He is God in His most minute and intimate aspects. He is God at work in us and available to us. In His own gentle way, He is always taking the initiative with us. The Holy Spirit is the Bringer of that grace, which flows from the love of God through the Cross of Christ, which restores and renews the life of man . . . He stands alongside to help . . . He guides . . . He convicts the world of sin . . . the Holy Ghost, the Comforter? Sometimes! But sometimes, The Holy Spirit, the Discomforter. Conviction may have to come before direction . . . He brings faith in Christ to another person . . . He brings unity and fellowship . . . St. Paul associates the Holy Spirit with varieties of spiritual gifts, saying "To each is given the manifestation of the Spirit for the common good."[4]

If we would answer the question 'Where is the Church?' we must ask 'Where is the Holy Spirit recognisably present with power?' "[5]

There can be no activity of prayer with any significance if the Holy Spirit is not at its heart.

References

1. Dietrich Bonhoeffer, *The Cost of Discipleship.*
2. Stephen Winward, *Teach Yourself to Pray* (Hodder & Stoughton), p.86.
3. Quoted by Stephen Winward in *Teach Us to Pray*, p.22.
4. S. Shoemaker, *With the Holy Spirit and With Fire*, pp. 45, 29-34.
5. Leslie Newbiggin, *The Household of God*, p.95.

6   Conversational Prayer

Most conventional prayer in small groups has been dull and lifeless because it has been a series of lengthy, drawn out orations. All too often people in group prayer have preached short sermons to each other instead of conversing with their Heavenly Father.

There has been an absence of mental discipline as the majority have not given thought to what they are saying. A long string of sentences have been used to say what could have been condensed into one or two sentences with a little thought. A friend of mine has a plaque which reads "Engage mind before opening mouth". Prayer would greatly benefit from that advice.

Also in so much collective prayer we have not shown a sensitivity to one another. Minds have wandered while others prayed, usually because the prayers were so lengthy. There has not been that love and respect for one another which should be characteristic of a Christian community.

Roslyn Rinker in *Communicating Love Through Prayer* and *Prayer and Conversing with God* has introduced a new approach to group prayer which for many has lifted it out of its lifelessness and brought a new reality.

Conversational prayer is this: Instead of each one present praying once and covering many subjects, each one prays as many times as he wishes. But he prays simple brief prayers for only one subject each time.

The purpose of conversational prayer is the real purpose of all true prayer — to put God at the centre of our attention, and forget ourselves and the impression we are making on others.

"It is conversation directed to God who is with us and within us, as well as to each other. It contains three ingredients common to any meaningful communication which are:

1. **We become aware** of the other person what they say, what they mean, how they feel.

2. **We pursue the same subject** by taking turns, listening, speaking, agreeing and giving thanks.

3. **We try to keep in tune** by not prematurely introducing a new subject, but by maintaining interest through participation in the current subject."

Conversational prayer is a group of brothers and sisters in real conversation with their Father. It involves silences in which we listen for God's response in our spirits, and, like real conversation, it means listening to what others are saying to Him.

It is speaking confidently, yet reverently, with a Person who really loves us and accepts us in Christ as we are. The conversation takes place in a group which is growing in love and concern for one another. This growth is not the fruit of their own effort, but the result of the action of the Holy Spirit.

Honesty, openness and simplicity with the One who really loves us and a group who accepts us is essential. But this will also be a growing experience. Part of that openness is saying "I" when we mean "I" and "we" when we mean the whole group.

Each may pray as many times as they wish but each short prayer relates to the subject being pursued by the group at that time. There is no order for people to follow, each prays as they feel moved by the Spirit.

Conversational prayer is an art which needs time and practice to develop. In our prayer workshops and in retreat situations I have found that even with people who have a real motivation to learn this prayer technique it has taken four half-hour workshops on successive days before most begin to gain some confidence in using it. Young people generally master the art more quickly than adults.

As Roslyn Rinker says: "Conversational prayer is loving sensitivity".

**The four
basic steps**

"There are Four Basic Steps of conversational prayer which form an easily recalled framework. They are as follows:

1. **Jesus is here**   The power of worship.
Realising God's presence.
Accepting God's love.
Matthew 18:19-20.

2. **Thank you Lord**   The power of thanksgiving.
Speaking from our hearts.
Freedom from fear.
Phil. 4:4-7.

3. **Help me Lord**   The power of confession.
Supporting and affirming one another.
Receiving love.
James 5:13-16.

4. **Help my brother**   The power of intercession.
Giving away our love.
Receiving answers.
Mark 11:22-25.

Notice the progression in the steps.

1. We start with our Lord and worship.
2. Gratitude opens our hearts and our mouths.
3. We pray for ourselves and for those present.
4. We include those who are not present."

**The fifth
basic step**

Joy Udy suggests a further basic step which brings a note of dedication and declaration of availability for involvement with others.

5. **Use me Lord**

It indicates a willingness to be part of the answer to our prayers of intercession.

The purpose of these steps is to give a starting point and a workable plan to follow. They help bring direction and meaning to group prayer. To follow them requires attention and thus produces fresh interest.

The five steps in more detail

1. Jesus is here. This begins usually with a period of silent meditation possibly following some of the suggestions for creative imagination in "Adoration" made in Chapter 5. The whole segment may be in silence but usually people will be motivated to verbalise their deep inner response to His presence. It helps for the leader to introduce this step by reciting Matthew 18:19, 20.

The reading of a very brief meditation which suggests the presence of Christ with the group can be helpful and bring variety. An appropriate symbol in the middle of the group can launch the group into meditation.

2. Thank you Lord. This is closely linked with the first step. It is the natural response to the awareness of the Presence of a loving God so rich in grace. A period of reflection to begin this segment may help, possibly using the suggestions made earlier under "Thanksgiving".

These first steps are a unit of worship in receiving love from God and responding in expressing our love and worship to Him. The next three steps are a giving of love to others both in the group and outside it. In step three there will be a beautiful experience in receiving love from one another as each person is supported and affirmed by other members of the group.

3. Help me Lord. In this step confession and petition are the focus. This follows easily after the study of the Word of God. Wise and sensitive leadership will be needed here. Until the group develops deeper levels of trust and openness we have found it best to suggest personal confession be in silence. (Again see the suggestions in chapter 5). Much will depend upon those in the group. However, normally a group should be expected to progress to open prayer in this step. Just be discerning and do not proceed too quickly. On no account should anyone feel coerced into doing what they are not ready to do. Sometimes the group can be broken into sub-groups of two or three at this stage. There will be a warmth in the fellowship as personal honesty and healing love are experienced.

144

4.   Help my brother. Here we enter into the power of intercession. It begins by responding to the individual prayers in "Step 3" and widens out to the families, friends and acquaintances of the group and to the community and world.

In explaining this step I find it clearer to divide it in two making a distinction between the response to individual prayers within the group and the wider intercession. The first part takes place spontaneously immediately after each person has prayed their prayers of confession and petition. The second part takes place as a further separate step.

(a)   Response during 'step 3' — Let Roslyn Rinker explain: "As soon as a person prays for themselves, another one or two should be applying a "band-aid" of love upon that wounded spirit. Any revealing of the heart calls for immediate response on the part of those who heard the prayer. Let your prayer-response be brief, to the point, with thanksgiving and with love. And without preaching or suggesting. Prayer should involve neither of these. We pray for each other by name, back and forth sometimes, according to the discernment received through listening and through loving. It is important that the group be small so first names — yes, first names — of those present are used. Prayer then becomes a more meaningful act of personal love and concern." The response may be for example, 'That's just how I feel too, Lord', 'I have just the same problem, Lord, help us both', or, 'Help Jim to know we love him'."

(b)   Intercession for other than group members. This segment will benefit from the suggestions made in chapter 5 under "Forms of Prayer". Let it be creative and specific. After one persons prays for a person or situation, one or two others in the group will support the prayer. In some cases the support prayers will be "Yes, Lord"; "That is our real concern, too, Lord"; "Lord, we share John's concern for his friend".

5.   Use me Lord. This is a natural progression for the sincerely concerned person. He sees that God does not do everything Himself in answer to our prayers. God chooses to work through people.

True intercessory prayer in the small group should lead to corporate and personal action in meeting the needs of others. A prayer group without a social conscience is a farce. Prayer and action make the finest combination for changing our world.

In this step we put a pair of legs under our prayers. We make ourselves available to be part of the answer "Lord, I'm available to bring your love and concern to Mrs. Jones who lost her husband last week"; "So am I Lord, guide us as to how we can best minister to her"; "Yes, Lord".

This will be followed, after the prayer time, by making definite plans to act upon the things the group felt moved to do during prayer.

In our involvement with people it will not always be possible or appropriate to actually be physically present. Sometimes our prayer "Use me Lord" will result in a continuing commitment to support that person in prayer. It may involve a telephone call or writing a letter.

The role of the leader

We have found it essential to have a sensitive leader in each group to facilitate this prayer experience. The leader will need to be conversant with the process and able to sense when it is appropriate to move on to the next stage. The leader will also need to know how to handle people who are negative, critical or unwise in sharing their personal failures.

Use of a visual aid

In our small groups the members have always been appreciative of a simple diagram which sets out the Five Steps and lists one or two of the main points. This has been given to each member to have on their lap during prayer. In our prayer workshops where a number of groups have been in a large hall a large poster or an overhead projector transparency of this diagram has been used. People need to be assured that they can feel free to open their eyes to refer to the diagram. (I cannot recall a direction in Scripture to close our eyes in prayer if we want God to hear us!) In some groups we have simply roneoed a list of the steps with appropriate Scriptures and a few brief comments under each step, which each person kept before them.

146

**Concluding the
prayer period**

In a single group this is no problem as the leader will take the initiative at the appropriate time. But where a cluster of groups are praying in the one situation I find it beneficial to play some quiet appropriate music on a cassette or player when the agreed time has been reached.

**It takes time
to learn**

Some people, especially more mature folk, find it extremely difficult to adapt themselves to this new form of prayer. All should be made aware that this is a skill which needs time and patience to develop. A few never seem to master it. Most will find it hard to keep to one subject at a time or restrict their prayers to one or two sentences. Save embarrassment by acknowledging this from the outset. Encourage them to persevere.

CONVERSATIONAL PRAYER

"Where two or three are gathered together in My name there am I in the midst of them."

- Be sensitive to each other — listen, be aware.
- Pursue the same subject.
- Move to new subject when leader suggests.
- Limit prayers to one or two sentences.
- Pray more than once.
- Be honest and open.
- Use "I" when mean "I", "we" when mean whole group.

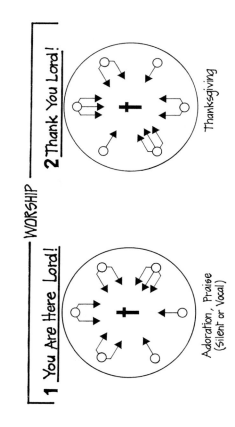

WORSHIP

1 You Are Here Lord!

Adoration, Praise
(Silent or Vocal)

2 Thank You Lord!

Thanksgiving

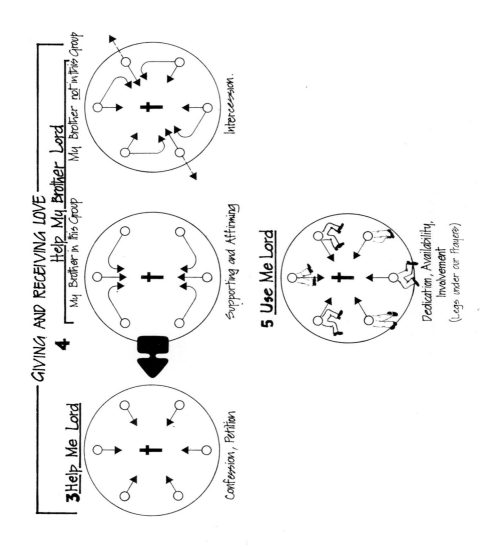

GIVING AND RECEIVING LOVE

Help My Brother Lord

My Brother in this Group   My Brother not in this Group

4

3 Help Me Lord

Intercession.

Supporting and Affirming

Confession, Petition

5 Use Me Lord

Dedication, Availability, Involvement
(Legs under our Prayers)

7 Creative Prayer Methods in Small Groups

For so many, group prayer has been a dull uninteresting exercise. To communicate with our Heavenly Father who loves us so deeply should be a fulfilling experience. God has given mankind the gift of creativity and imagination and this rich endowment should be used to make prayer a lively, varied, satisfying activity.

These methods and ideas are given as suggestions which should be adapted to each situation. Not everyone will find each item helpful. Therefore they will need to be used with discretion.

SPOKEN PRAYERS

We have already dealt with **conversational prayer** in detail in the previous chapter. Many have found a whole new dimension to their group prayer experiences through following this method.

Enabling spontaneous prayer

Spontaneous spoken prayer may be a frightening experience. Some people like to have time to "think out" their prayer if praying in a group with others, while others may be so afraid of their own voice that they never have the courage to speak. As an aid to spontaneous praying, a leader may encourage members by asking the group for a few suggestions of people or topics to include in the prayer, and then formulate these into prayer. Or, the leader may suggest that he/she will open and close in prayer and ask the group members to just say aloud their point or person for prayer. The leader should try to keep the prayer simple in order to encourage others that praying aloud is something anyone can do. One needs to remember also that spontaneous praying is a basis for an adult relationship with God and not all people have attained this maturity — some may be "on the way".

Chain prayer

Chain prayer involves each person praying in order around the group. Its main drawback is that people can feel forced to pray, resulting in embarrassment. However this can be avoided by stressing the validity of silent prayer. Those who wish to pray in silence can just touch the next person when they have completed their silent prayer or, if not wishing to pray. Chain prayer can be used for each segment of prayer going around the circle once or twice for the period of Adoration, then around the chain again for Thanksgiving and so on. Confession is generally in silence with each indicating when they have concluded. It is often used for one segment only with a different procedure for the other aspects.

One word bombardments

These are helpful in encouraging those who are new to group prayer. Each spends a brief period in silent reflection and follows this with a prayer focused into one word or a brief phrase. For example, in adoration, time may be spent in meditation upon an attribute of God or the promise of Christ's presence in the group. The group responds as each feels moved, with "Jesus", "Father", "Our Lord", "You are here", "We adore you", etc. It is especially helpful for Adoration and Thanksgiving. When used for Intercession the person's name only is used, or the specific situation mentioned.

Litany response

In this a prepared prayer is used with a copy for each to follow. The leader reads brief portions which are followed with prepared responses for the whole group to read. These are readily available in older or modern forms. Copies of The Book of Common Prayer or the recently published Australian revision or other equivalents could be borrowed or roneoed copies of certain sections made. A number of hymns, old and modern, lend themselves for this use, e.g. 'Jesus with Thy Church Abide" and "Saviour, when in dust to Thee". The chorus of others can be used as the response or the last line or two adapted. Some groups write their own litany as the follow-up from a study, which is then used to conclude the group meeting.

Bidding prayers

The leader needs a book of prayers prepared for this purpose or a list is compiled, either by the leader beforehand, or by the group during the meeting. The leader then bids, or invites the group, "Let us remember God's goodness to us", or "Let us pray for our government" which is followed by silent or vocal response by the members. The leader may pray a brief prayer on the subject before moving on to the next point. The leadership can be shared with any number of members, each taking a different aspect.

Open-eyed prayer

We have been taught to close our eyes in prayer to help our concentration. It has become a rigid ritual unfortunately, "All eyes closed . . .". Occasionally try keeping your eyes open and focussing on a symbol, or worship centre or picture of the creation and respond in prayer. This works especially well when the group is able to meet in a bushland or garden setting or overlooking the sea.

Often when we discuss persons and situations for intercession in order to prepare a list of requests to follow, the time quickly slips away and someone in a surprised voice says, "Oh! We have run out of time and will not have time for intercession!" It does well to remember where God was during the conversation! He heard every word. A brief prayer acknowledging God's presence during the "open-eyed conversation" and committing to Him all that was mentioned can then be prayed without the group feeling their concerned conversation was wasted.

WRITTEN PRAYER

Group prayer is an art which many find difficult to launch into. Older folk who have not prayed openly particularly find it a traumatic experience. Beginners in corporate prayer often benefit from writing out a prayer and then reading it when the group prays. A natural way to do this is in response to a study period. Each participant writes their own prayer, which they then read in the group. However, people should still be given the opportunity to not participate.

Some wise leaders have suggested to a person who is experiencing this difficulty that they prepare a prayer at home which they may be asked to read to open the group or in the collective prayer sessions.

Paraphrasing

Paraphrasing traditional prayers or hymns is a useful exercise. A prayer from the Bible, a book of prayers or a hymn-prayer, is re-written by each individual. It is kept simple by using everyday words. A dictionary for each participant will help in putting technical words in a way each would say it. With long prayers or hymns assign segments around the group. This work can also be done as a home assignment. The paraphrases are then read in group prayers.

Re-writing the 23rd Psalm

Psalm 23 would be the best known of all psalms but is written in terms with which we are not very familiar in our nuclear age. Shepherd and sheep had a close relationship and that association had far more meaning when the psalm was written. Try re-writing the psalm in modern English (or Australian!) using comparisons with which people are familiar. In *God is for Real, Man,* by Carl Burke (Fontana, 1967), the paraphrase of the 23rd Psalm says that the Lord is like a 'probation officer' — that term had special relevance for kids from the streets. Perhaps terms such as "navigator", "companion" etc. might be used. The idea is for the participants to choose a word that is their model of God. Having done that, move through the psalm, changing the ideas to whatever is relevant, keeping in mind the picture of God that was chosen, then allow the psalm to be a prayer of affirmation and confidence in God.

Personalize and update the Lord's Prayer

While recognizing the Lord's Prayer is given to us in the plural so that it embraces all peoples, a fresh approach may be taken when we pause to personalize it. Take all words written in the plural and substitute "My Father", "me" throughout, and also replace old-fashioned words such as "art", "hallowed" etc. with words current in the vocabulary of today. After having discussed the changes in the group, pray the prayer quietly to oneself.

Dialogue prayer

This is a way of holding a real conversation with God. Feelings are expressed without pretence. Each person writes out their prayer, recording what they say to God together with what they imagine God to be saying in reply.

154

When we are in a close relationship with a person we can closely predict what their expected response might be. God has revealed His character to us in the Scriptures. We know sufficient about Him to have some ideas concerning the replies we could expect from Him.

Let the conversation flow back and forth until you feel the dialogue has finished. It is kept brief and precise. What each person imagines God to be saying must be consistent with His nature and intentions revealed in Scripture and supremely through the Lord Jesus Christ.

THE USE OF SILENCE

Silence plays an important part in private and corporate prayer. People need encouragement and help in spending more time in silent meditation and contemplation "Be still and **know** that I am God" is a wise word for busy people in the 20th century. **Planned silence** should be a regular part of all group prayer. Until the group develops an ability to use the silences it should be kept reasonably short. Suggestions may need to be fed in from time to time.

Some help should be given in using **unplanned silence.** When the group is praying verbally and a silence occurs teach the group to continue to use the time in non-verbal prayer or listen for the voice of God speaking to their souls.

TOUCHING OR PHYSICAL CONTACT

Most of us know the power of touch — a friendly slap on the back, a hug, a warm handshake; the gentle, loving touch of our closest loved one; a child's arms thrown around us in a spontaneous welcome; a concerned friend's arms around our shoulder in a time of distress.

Jesus touched people to heal and bless them. His followers have found the human touch in prayer to be important. Some will have reservations and others real problems in being touched by another but it is often very supportive to hold a person's hand as we pray for him or her. As in Jesus' ministry, somehow power is transmitted person to person by touch.

Laying on of hands

This is an ancient tradition practised by Jesus, the early church, and used frequently since, for setting apart persons for special ministries and for healing. In small groups it is commonly used when praying for one who has openly expressed a deep desire for special prayer for personal renewal, or for healing, or a fuller awareness of the Spirit, and to acknowledge special gifts or to confirm a person's call to a specific task. The members of the group gather around the person and lay their hands on his head, shoulders or back.

Sometimes "laying on of hands" by **proxy** has great meaning. A person in the group "stands-in" for one who is not present, the others laying their hands on him. The "proxy" person seeks to become one with the person for whom prayer is being offered.

Huddles

These can give a sense of concern for each member and deepen the sense of unity. All stand in a tight circle with shoulders touching. Arms can be placed on each other's shoulders or around waists, or hands held.

Cradling

This can be a supportive caring experience for someone who has shared deeply and seeks the group's care and concern in their problem. The person lies on his or her back on the floor. The group gathers around, then lifts the person to waist height and rocks him or her back and forth like a baby. Prayers may be spoken for the person while he or she is cradled. Usually a minimum of four persons on either side is needed. The process concludes by standing the person back on their feet.

BODY POSITION kneeling

This has traditionally been a common pose for prayer. It is an indication of humility and submission to our Sovereign God. For physical reasons not everyone will be able to kneel and when it is done for long periods some will find it more difficult than others. The pose can be varied by facing inward during most of the prayer period and changing to face outward during the period of intercession as an indication of concern for others outside the immediate group. Most people will find it helpful to have a chair or table to rest against if the period is to be prolonged.

Lying prostrate

This is seldom done in prayer today but it was a common pose in the Bible as an indication of complete submission to God. Young people have used this in recent times with benefit.

Reclining

Reclining is a relaxed position. A chapel in a retreat centre I visited had an inspiring art piece in the ceiling. The absence of any seating and a carpeted floor was a natural setting for this relaxed form of meditation and prayer.

The wheel position

This is a more structured form of reclining for a small group to experience a restful unity. The group lie on the floor to form a wheel with heads facing inwards, each person being a spoke! Hands are raised and grasped and prayer made together with a deep sense of oneness.

Creative movement

Dancing

Dancing has played an important part in the worship of God. The Old Testament tells of Miriam and the women with timbrels and dancing singing praise to God *(Exodus 15:20, 21)*; *"David danced before the Lord" (2 Samuel 6:14)* and the Psalms contain exhortations to *"Praise His name with dancing" (Ps. 149:3)* and *praise him with timbrel and dance" (Ps. 150:4)*. Not everyone will feel sufficiently uninhibited to participate in dance so it will need to be used with sensitivity and as an optional prayer response.

Some groups play appropriate recorded hymns, songs or music to which each individual can make their own prayer response combined with dance.

Non-verbal body prayers

These are used to amplify a prayer through body motion. The group stand at more than arm's length from each other with eyes closed. As the leader slowly recites the Lord's Prayer or another appropriate prayer or hymn, each expresses the thoughts by appropriate body movement.

FANTASIZING

This is a creative use of our God-given gift of imagination in prayer. Taking a similar position to the non-verbal body prayers each person seeks to identify with the creation by playing a **fantasy role.** While background music is playing and eyes are closed each imagines that they are a mountain stream, a cloud, a flower, a water-lily on a pond, a leaf or a tree. After a few minutes prayers are offered stemming from the feelings experienced.

These are used regularly in therapy and can be put **Fantasy trips** to good use by a sensitive leader in group prayer. We have found it particularly helpful in confession or in thanksgiving. Each sits or lies (if there is room) in a comfortable relaxed manner with eyes closed. Through centering their thoughts on their breathing they seek to get in touch with themselves. Slow deep breathing helps the relaxation. After a brief period the leader asks each to imagine that they are lying relaxed on a carpet. It is a magic carpet which slowly lifts them up and gently conveys them through past events and experiences. The leader reinforces this movement backward into the past, by: "What were you doing before you came tonight — was there anything for which you can be genuinely thankful?" "Where were you today?" "Who were you with?" "What did you do?" "What did you see?" "Can you recall something for which you can praise God?" And so back over the last few days and then let them go back as far as they wish into their past till they recall a person, an event for which they can truly be thankful to God. The "trip" needs to be completed with a bringing back to the present and a brief period of relaxation for de-roling. When used for confession a segment for specific handing over of guilt and acceptance of forgiveness by faith must be followed by assurance of forgiveness, together with some reassuring acts within the group each to the other. A brief period of sharing can conclude the experience which will give opportunity to share any disturbing memories or feelings and inspiring or enriching recollections. The sharing could be introduced with "How do you feel after that experience?" Most leaders need training in this form of prayer.

Too much group prayer is vague, especially when it **PRAYER** comes to promises to pray for each other. The small group **CONTRACTS** movement in Pittsburgh, known as the Pittsburgh Experiment, uses **the 30 Day Experiments** as one of its main emphases for individual and group prayer. In one of their pamphlets it is explained:

"A thirty day experiment is simply this. We suggest that no matter what the problem or concern might be, if a person will only pray every day, as often as he thinks about it or feels tension arise within himself, that God will help him to understand the situation and the other parties involved. We have seen this work in hundreds of situations. I have yet to see anyone who has been faithful and honest in daily prayer for thirty days, end up with their prayers unanswered."

The group can enter into a contract with a person to pray for any specific period — 7 days, 14 days or 30 days. It avoids vague promises of support and encourages concentrated prayer for a specific period at the end of which progress can be shared.

PRAYER AIDS
Small cards

These could be approximately 130 mm by 80 mm (standard file cards are useful). They can be written on without needing a support and fit into the back of an average size Bible. Use them for each person to note the intercessory prayer requests for the day. Each may send their card around the group so that others may write a signed prayer request on it and return it to the owner as a reminder throughout the week to pray for the group. It has a variety of other uses.

Prayer record
books

We found it useful to use a cheap school exercise book to record the requests for prayer in an intercessory prayer group. A separate page was kept for each meeting with the opposite page kept free for recording progress in answers to prayer at future meetings. From time to time it was an inspiring experience of thanksgiving and praise to look back over the months and recall God's answers to our prayers:

Hymn book

A hymn book is a rich prayer resource for private and corporate prayer. For the non-conformist churches it is their prayer book. Many hymns are written in the form of a prayer. Use them for reciting together or silent meditation. Sing or read them as prayers. Let the leader slowly and prayerfully read a verse or so of a hymn of "adoration" to commence the prayer time. In a time of "confession" each may read in silence a hymn of "repentance and forgiveness''. Sing together a hymn of thanksgiving. Paraphrase a hymn, putting it into your own words. The group members could each take a book and find a prayer that is meaningful for them; or a hymn could be chosen for the group, the words of which could be duplicated or hand printed on chart paper, and members asked to choose a verse as their special prayer for that day.

Books of prayers

There are many books of ancient and contemporary prayers which can be read or studied or paraphrased by the group. John Bailey's *Diary of Private Prayer* can be adapted for group prayer, *Worship and Wonder* by E. S. P. Jones contains a good variety of prayers. Michael Quoist has a number of books of contemporary prayers; *Great Souls at Prayer* by Mary W. Tileston (Allenson & Co., 1899-1963) is a treasury of ancient and more recent prayers.

Newspapers

These are useful in making intercession specific. Give each member a news page of a recent daily newspaper. Allow time for them to select a news item for prayer and underline the main points. Each gives a summary of the news item which is followed by group prayer. Or each can write a prayer in response to the news item they chose. These are then read in the group prayer time.

A variation would be to give each person a newspaper and ask them to choose an item that is of interest. (It may be a story, report, advertisement or cartoon). Now ask, what is the relation between the article you've chosen and God?

Having established the connection, form a prayer around the theme. For example, with an advertisement designed to sell cars the prayer may include thanks for all those involved in the production and design of same. Intercession for those working on the repetitive production line; for migrant workers; for those injured in producing vehicles; a prayer for responsibility for those who drive, intercession for those who have been injured in a car accident. These could be made more specific — we can pray for a realization of our own responsibilities on social issues — it is not enough to pray that there will be no strikes — think about what causes are involved.

Symbols

These have played an important part in giving a common focus, stimulating reflection and facilitating a worship response to God. A cross, candle, loaf of bread, chalice, jug of water, open Bible, vacant chair, or a simple drawing of a fish or dove, and other traditional symbols can be useful aids if they are varied.

The Creation

The world around us is rich with things to inspire our prayers. Ask each member of the group to bring some natural object with them to the next meeting. (This could be a banksia flower, a piece of driftwood, a stone, etc.) Alternatively, if it is a day meeting (and depending on the locality) each person could go out and find an article. In any case, they are asked to conceal it so the others do not see what they have. Arrange the group in pairs numbering A and B, then ask A to close his/her eyes while B puts the "found object" he/she has brought into A's hand. A feels the article, may smell it or even taste it while trying to guess what it is. When that has been done, A then gives to B what he/she has brought.

While each partner still holds the article which the other person has brought, ask each to try and imagine that piece of nature in its original state. Then ask "Does it remind one of God in any way?" Following a short period of silence ask each to use their picture image as the basis for a personal prayer.

If the object brought to the group was a rock it may have reminded the person of the strength and stability of Christ's love — "He is my rock and fortress", etc.

Members **may** like to share with one another their thoughts which led to the foundation of their prayer.

THE BIBLE

The Bible will be our most useful aid to group prayer. Here we find many prayers of the patriarchs, prophets, psalmist, our Lord and the apostles. The Christian's understanding of prayer comes primarily from this book. Studies of the teaching and example of Jesus and the apostles will be an important aid to group prayer. The recorded prayers can be paraphrased, personalised or used as they are.

Keep eyes and ears open for music, songs, an excerpt from a book, TV or radio commercial, poem, etc. which may either form a prayer in itself or be an excellent opener for one. An example of each:

(a) "Father, we're all gone far away, we have spent all, we are poor, we are tired of it all, we want to feel different, to be different. We want to come back. Jesus came to save us from our sins and He said if we came He wouldn't cast us out, no matter how bad we were, if only we came back to Him. Oh, Jesus Christ, we are a poor lot, and we are trying to find the way. Show us how to get back, Amen." (The camp renegade in "Black Rock" by Ralph Connor).

(b) As an "opener" to prayer, play a record of "My Favourite Things" from "Sound of Music", then ask each person to list, say, ten of their favourite things and then move into prayer of Thanksgiving. Or, it may be a topical song chosen, leading to prayers of intercession.

GENERAL
What are the words saying?

There are reminders of God all around us. Choose four objects and suggest they be the basis for prayer, or ask each person to contribute an object. One may choose a pair of glasses, a dictionary, map of the world, a coin and the prayer could be "Enlarge my vision, O Lord, to see meaning in the ordinary and the profound and extend my vision to perceive the needs of others round about me. Remind me there is a tangible way of helping those less fortunate than I am."

God in everyday things

Ask each to choose as a partner the person sitting next to them, and explain that they will be given 30 seconds to think of someone, or some need in the world, for which they would like to pray. (This could be varied by asking them to think of a problem which they wouldn't mind sharing with their partner; or, think of someone who means a lot to them.) Allow about 30 seconds for each to explain to his/her partner the prayer need.

Then remind the group of Jesus' promise that where two or three are gathered in His name there He is in the midst (Matt. 18:20) and that in the **silence** of the next 30 seconds each will be asked to remember that promise and to pray for the need that their partner has just shared with them.

Share a prayer

162

Appreciation of love

A good introduction to this method would be to play the record "Where is Love" from the musical "Oliver". There are an abundance of relevant songs on this theme. Take a sheet of paper and across the top write:
"THANK YOU, GOD, FOR YOUR LOVE AS I SEE IT EXPRESSED ALL AROUND ME".
Underneath make four columns with the following headings: A place I've loved; An animal who loved me; People who have loved me; and People I love. Think carefully and try to picture in one's mind the names and places that immediately come into view. Describe the place, be it home, town, church, bushland, etc. Do the same with the animal. Go back in life and move forward as you recall those who have loved you and those you have loved.

Use your list now as you pray quietly, thanking God for the love you have experienced in the past, present — and the future. (Prior to this last step, each group member might like to share one point from their list.)

Expressing thanksgiving

Give to each member a sheet of paper and pencil, asking that the paper be divided in these sections — across the top allow a two inch margin and underneath to be divided into four upright columns.

THANK YOU GOD FOR THE GOOD THINGS OF ....19....
(Use today's date if evening meeting, otherwise date previous day)

Good Things I Did	People I Enjoyed Being With	Good Experiences (things that happened to me.)	Good Reminders of You (God)

A time of silence is allowed while each person completes the sheet. **Then suggest that each re-reads what they have** written, thanking God for what they have been enabled to write.

Another way of thanksgiving — cut coloured paper or gift wrapping paper in rectangles and decorate so each resembles a parcel. Distribute one to each person (together with a pencil or texta) and ask that they write down a gift/s which God has given them, for which they are especially grateful, and which they don't mind the other group members seeing. Then using a board, ask each to come forward and place the gift parcel on it (with pin or masking tape). The leader may ask if the gifts suggest a prayer. The members may then move to a time of Thanksgiving, or one member may praise, using the names on the gifts.

Removing mountains

Ask the group to look up Matthew 17:20. Remind members that Jesus placed an emphasis on **faith** as the condition of appropriating God's love and power. Prepare several small cards (about 130 mm by 80 mm) and give one to each person. Explain that they are to write the "mountain" which he/she is facing at the moment on the card and that this will become known to the group later. Their name is **not** to be on the paper. When each has finished, the cards are collected, shuffled and distributed to the members.

Silently the person reads the other person's "mountain" and prays for that mountain to be removed. Then each card is read aloud, the group pausing after the reading of each for quiet prayer.

Doodle praying

Having given each person pencil and paper, ask each to doodle (aimless drawing such as those we often do while we are talking on the telephone!) whatever comes into their mind. Use the doodle as a prayer opener. For example, one doodle might be

in which case the prayer might be

"Lord, when I see these squares, it reminds me of that song "Little Boxes" and I think of all those who see the place in which they live as a box and not a home. For those who live in large blocks of flats and whose freedom is restricted we pray this day . . ."

One person may be prepared to draw their doodle on a flip chart or board where each may see and that doodle then becomes the prayer opener for the group.

"Doodles" have almost limitless forms:—

8 Relationship Games for Small Groups

Introduction

One of the exciting things about the Small Group movement is the way in which people have found new and deeper levels in their relationships to each other. Relating to one another; sharing ourselves, our feelings, our faith, doubts and knowledge are all factors for growing as a Christian. Thus it is that we can find the two way relationship from which we can only benefit and grow to be what Jesus knows we can be.

Relationship is a strong Biblical concept. We do well to avail ourselves of the tools to make the most offered by this concept. These group games are only a sample of the variety of games available. A number of books of games readily available are listed in the resources section in Book No. 4.

We have omitted in-depth games such as those used in encounter or T-group situations as these require special leadership skills. However, even in the use of most of the games described, there is a need for sensitivity as relationships can be spoilt and individuals hurt. No one should feel coerced into participating in any activity or anything they do not wish to do.

We have not included any Simulation Games as these are covered in books such as *Using Simulation Games*, published by the Joint Board of Christian Education, Melbourne.

CONTENTS

GET-ACQUAINTED GAMES

These games are used to help people in the early part of their group experience. They are designed to help them feel comfortable, included and significant. They also will provide one of the first important steps in group involvement, that of hearing their own voice and being listened to by the group.

INTERVIEWS

A completely non-threatening game, of value when commencing a new group or for one-time small group meetings.

Purpose:

This is a "warming up" period which should create a congenial emotional climate. It also provides the opportunity for every person to say something early in the meeting. It is important for people to hear their own voices. This makes people feel they are "in the act", that they count, are wanted and respected.

Also sharing something of themselves in this manner should open the way for them to share at a deeper level later in the meeting.

Setting:

Small groups with even numbers of people. Upper limit of 12 people. Can be used with larger groups, but more time is required.

Time:

Depends upon the number in group. Usually takes **approximately 25 minutes** for a group of 12.

Materials required:

Jotter pads and pencils — one per pair.

Procedure:

Distribute pencils and small writing pads for brief notes taken in the interviews. Briefly explain the method. **Pair off the group,** being sure that married couples or close friends are not put together. With the assistance of a number of **suggested questions one seeks to discover as much as possible about the other in 2 to 3 minutes. The process is then reversed for a similar period.**

Each person in turn then shares with the whole group what he has learned about the other.

The method of introducing the questions will vary:

— They may be put on a chart and placed in a prominent position for all to see.
— They may be dictated for the group to copy down individually — (this is time consuming).
— They may be typed out (or roneoed) for each person with sufficient room left for the answers.

Most people will need a set of questions to give direction, and breadth to their interview.

Questions for interviews

Suggested questions: Name?

Where do you live?
How long have you been living there?
Where were you born?
Occupation?
Married — Family?
Interests — Hobbies?
　　　　　　Sport?
　　　　　　Clubs?
What is the nicest thing that happened to you in the last 12 months?

These will need to be adjusted for use in **groups for young people.** Some possible inclusions could be:

Which school do you attend?
How many in your family?
What is your favourite TV show?

(See Section "Questions and Suggestions for Sharing" for more questions from which you can select.)

170

WARM UP

Purpose: To help a new group to get to know each other and provide an opportunity for some sharing of spiritual experience.

Setting: A circle with each person in the group able to see the face of every other person.

Time: **Approximately 60 minutes.**

Materials required: None.

Procedure: The leader explains to the group, "We are going to take a few minutes to get acquainted. In order to do this we are going to ask ourselves several questions. These questions are not 'loaded' questions but simply represent a way we have found to get to know each other in a short time."

Questions:

Step 1

(1) What is your name?

(2) Where did you live between the ages of seven and twelve years?

(3) What stands out most in your mind about the school you attended?

The leader proceeds to answer the first then goes completely around the circle asking each person to answer the question.

Step 2

(1) How many brothers and sisters were in your family during the ages seven to twelve years?

(2) During your childhood, how was your home heated? Can you remember anything humorous about it?

Leaders, in telling about how their homes were heated, should try to think of some incident that may be humorous or vivid concerning the heat in their homes (perhaps being cold in the morning, or having to get up and fetch the wood).

Step 3

During that time where did you feel the centre of human warmth was? Was it a room or a person? (e.g. the kitchen, parents' bedroom, dining room, etc.) Or it may not have been a room at all; it may have been a person around whom in retrospect you sensed an aura of safeness or warmth.

At this point the leader can explain that what we are actually doing is tracing the human experience of security. Security is first known by a child in terms of physical warmth. As his horizon broadens outside of his immediate self, he senses his security in the warmth and acceptance of the people around him. (It is good to note that some people simply do not have any remembrance of a centre of human warmth in their home or in any person. The leader by mentioning this may put at ease people for whom this experience is not a reality.)

Step 4

This is asked to the group as a whole so that people can volunteer answers if they have any. This step can be optional as it may be construed as threatening by someone who is afraid to reveal himself or herself. The question is:

"When, if ever, in your life did God become more than 'a word'? When did He become a living Being, alive in your own thinking?"

We are not asking necessarily for an account of a conversion experience. This transition in one's thinking may have taken place while listening to a beautiful piece of music, watching a sunset, or in a conversation with a person who loved Him. By this time the group may know each other well enough to volunteer answers right away. If not, the leader tells of his own experience.

After this last question has been asked, the group is in the midst of a discussion on the reality of God in human life. And the leader may close this conversation by summarising the discussion and pointing out that, according to Christian belief, although everyone's experience of security and acceptance begins with physical warmth and graduates to human warmth, we are so made that our security will never be complete until we find it in God.

What this whole discussion does is to take people as a group of strangers, and within an hour's time get them talking personally with deep involvement about the deepest issues of human life.

GUESS WHO FISHBOWL

Purpose: To have fun getting to know each other in a history-giving guessing game that surfaces significant facts in your lives. This game frequently helps people realize how little they really know about fellow group members or surprises them by demonstrating how misleading it is to "typecast" or categorize people.

Setting: **Groups of eight** sitting in movable chairs or on the floor.

Time: **30 minutes.**

Materials required: A small sheet of paper and pencil for everyone, plus a bowl for each group of eight.

Procedure: The exercise is in two parts: (1) **Preliminary Exercise**—with everyone working on his own; and (2) **Guessing Game**—with everyone in groups of eight.

Preliminary Exercise (5 Minutes)

1. Give everyone **a sheet of paper** and ask them to **jot down four facts about themselves.** (Do not let anyone see what you jot down.)
   - (a) Your favourite radio or TV programme when you were a child.
   - (b) Your hero when you were twelve years of age.
   - (c) The place where you would like to spend a vacation.
   - (d) One word that would best describe your life right now.

2. **Fold your sheet of paper when you are finished.**

Note to Leader: With this much instruction, give everyone a sheet of paper and pencil and ask them to proceed. After 5 minutes, call time and proceed.

Guessing Game (25 minutes)

1. **Get together in groups of eight and place your sheet of paper in the bowl for your group.**

2. Let **one person pick out one of the slips** of paper and **read the four facts** or clues to the group. Then, **let everyone try to guess who it is. (The person who is "it" should play along** by guessing someone else.) **When everyone has tried to guess, let the person who is "it" confess and explain his or her answers.**

3. **Repeat this procedure** until you have removed all of the slips from the fishbowl.

4. If time allows — have a **general discussion** on what the game revealed.

IDENTITY CARD

Purpose:
To enable people in a large gathering to establish contact with a significant number of people not previously known to them.

To help people feel accepted and included.

To break a large group into smaller groups in a non-threatening manner.

Time:
20 to 30 Minutes

Setting:
Useful in larger gathering but can be used with smaller numbers.

Materials:
5 x 3 file cards — or scrap card cut to size. Pencils.

Procedure:
Distribute cards and pencils — one per person.

The leader selects a set of questions similar to those used in the "Interview" game.

These questions are presented as incomplete statements and read out by the leader. Each individual writes the statement plus his completion of it. (e.g. My occupation is . . .)

All of the statements are limited to the one side of the card.

All move around during a 15 minute period meeting as many as possible, especially those who they have not met before or are not well known to them.

During these encounters, cards are exchanged, the statements read, hands shaken and a welcome given by each. Then **each writes on the back of the other person's card a greeting or wish for the other and the writer's name signed.** (e.g. "I hope this will be a growing experience. Bill S.". "So nice to meet you. May God continue to enrich your life, Jill A.").

Cards are returned but the side with the greeting is **not** read at this stage.

Repeat this experience with as many as possible in the time available.

When the time expires, the pairs talking at that time sit together.

Only then are all the greetings, etc. on the reverse side of the card are read by the owner.

HUMMING BIRDS (AND FELLA'S!)

Purpose:
To facilitate contact between all members of a large group in a related climate of fun and humour.

To break a large group into smaller groups in a non-threatening manner.

Time:
Approximately **30 minutes.**

Materials:
A folded strip of paper with the title of a well-known song for each member of the group (one set of song title strips for each sub-group desired).

Procedure:
The leader commences in a light-hearted manner stating that there is a great deal of talent and skill in the room which will be made evident through this exercise. **Each is given a piece of paper on which is written the title of a well-known song.** Each looks at the title but does not share it with anyone else.

When the leader gives the word, each person will move around the room humming their tune until they find all of the other members of the group with the same song.

Suggested songs
"Waltzing Matilda", "Advance Australia Fair", "Three Blind Mice", "Auld Lang Syne", "Happy Birthday", "Kum Bah Yah", "For He's a Jolly Good Fellow".

When the groups have been formed, each group sits in a circle. Groups are instructed to discuss how they felt beginning and during the exercise, how they felt when they found the first group member and how they felt when their sub-group was completely identified.

If time permits, the total group is reassembled to share its feelings and expectations.

Variations
1. The leader can tell the participants how many others have the same song. This will accelerate the activity.
2. Instead of one song per strip, several songs can be listed. For example: (1) "Mary Had a Little Lamb". (2) "Jingle Bells". (3) "Waltzing Matilda". The first song is used to form dyads, the second song quartets, and the third a task group of any number for some later activity.
3. Group members can be assigned the task of coming up with a group name or a song title to express their feeling as a group.

GET-ACQUAINTED MERRY-GO-ROUND

Purpose: To get to know each other at the beginning of a course or conference or retreat.

Setting: Movable chairs or **sit on the floor in two concentric circles — the inner circle facing the outer circle. Note:** Divide the group first into **groups of eight;** and then **each group of eight into an inner and outer group.**

Time: 45 minutes.

Leader's note: The leader should complete the first three sentences, setting the pace for openness and honesty by his or her answers.

Procedure: The exercise is in two parts: **Merry-Go-Round** — with the outer circle in each group rotating every two minutes; and (2) **Synthesis** — with each group of eight together.

Merry-Go-Round (30 Minutes)

1. **Get together in groups of eight** and arrange the chairs or sit on the floor in a merry-go-round pattern — with **four people** in an **inner circle** and **four people** in an **outer circle.** The inner circle should face the outer circle in each group so that **everyone is facing a partner.**

2. **The leader will read the first part of a sentence and give you two minutes to finish the sentence and discuss your answer with the person you are facing.** Then, the leader will call time and ask **the people in the outer circle** to **rotate to the right.**

3. When you are settled in front of your new partner, the **leader will read out the next sentence** and let **you finish** the sentence and **discuss** your answer with your partner **for two more minutes. Then,** the leader will call time and ask you to **rotate again.**

4. **Continue this procedure** until you have **finished the sentences or have run out of time.**

(a) My favourite time in the day is . . .

(b) My favourite time in the year is . . .

(c) My favourite place in the house is . . .

(d) My favourite television show is . . .

(e) If I could visit any place in the world on a vacation, I would like to visit . . .

(f) If I had ten million dollars to use for the benefit of mankind, I would use the money to . . .

(g) If I could smash one thing and one thing only, I would smash . . .

(i) The greatest force in the history of the world is . . .

(j) The greatest crime one man can commit against another is . . .

(k) The greatest discovery I would like to make is . . .

(l) The greatest value in my life at the moment is . . .

(m) The thing that gives me the greatest satisfaction is . . .

(n) The thing that I fear the most is . . .

(o) The time I feel most alone is . . .

(p) The time I feel most alive is . . .

Synthesis (15 Minutes)

1. **Stay in your same group of eight,** but arrange your chairs or sit on the floor in one circle, **facing each other.**

2. **Go around and let each person finish the first sentence below and explain why. Then,** go around a **second** and **third time, until** you have **finished** the sentences **or your time has run out—**

   (a) The person I learned the most about in the last few minutes is . . .
   (b) The answer that surprised me most was . . .
   (c) The person in this group who seems most to feel about life the way I do is . . .

A SHORTER GET-ACQUAINTED MERRY-GO-ROUND

Purpose: As for Get-Acquainted Merry-Go-Round.

Setting: Up to eight people in each group.

Time: Up to thirty minutes.

Leader's Note: The leader should answer the first sentence then rotate from the right or left for the remaining three. This will help to show that the group members have very little, if anything, to fear from the sharing process.

Materials required: Biro/pencil and a sheet of paper for each person.

Procedure:

1. The leader asks the group to write down their answers to the following four statements:

   a. My favourite time of the day is.................................

   b. My favourite season of the year is.........................

   c. My favourite spot in the house is..........................

   d. If money were no object, the place I would most like to go for a holiday is.................................

2. As for point 2 (under "Synthesis") in longer version and if the leader feels that there is advantage to be gained, then he or she should allow the group to proceed to points (a), (b), (c).

3. The leader checks how the group members are feeling about sharing something of themselves, then concludes by making observations as to how they have shared some important feelings about themselves and yet have not been threatened. That is a part of the positive experiences of a Christian group.

QUESTIONS AND SUGGESTIONS FOR SHARING

The following questions and suggestions help facilitate sharing in small groups. They should be valuable in get-acquainted exercises. Many are in the values clarification area. (We are grateful to the Faith at Work staff for making available most of the material in the last three segments.)

Awareness of God (Right relationship to God)
1. What impresses you most about Jesus Christ?
2. What event in the life of Christ means the most to you?
3. In what ways does the creation inspire you?
4. When did God become real to you?
5. Who helped you most in your understanding of God?
6. When you were a child (or a teenager) what impressed you most about God?
7. Of all the things you know about the nature or character of God what means most to you personally?
8. When do you feel closest to God?
9. What one question above all others do you want God to answer?
10. If God is real to you what gives you that certainty?
11. What do you most want God to do for you?
12. What does "faith" mean to you personally?
13. When has God seemed furthest away from you?
14. What do you find hardest to believe about God?
15. "God is love" — what does that mean to you personally?
16. Of all the teachings of Jesus Christ what has come to be most significant in your life?
17. How do you endeavour to show your gratitude to God?
18. A word which best describes God to me is . . .
19. At what time in your life was God most real to you?
20. What is the most vivid experience of prayer you have had?
21. What certainty do you have that you matter to God?
22. In what way does your relationship to God make your way of facing life any different?

Self-Awareness, Right relationship to self
1. Draw your own crest or coat-of-arms as you wish it were (which describes you) . . . and explain it to the group.

179

2. What would you do if you knew you couldn't fail?
3. What would you most like to do or be for the next five years if there were no limitations (of family, money, education, health, etc.)?
4. Who is the most authentic person you have met? (Describe him/her.
5. What is your most satisfying accomplishment — ever? Before you were 6? between the ages of 6 and 12? 12 and 18? and 25? over 25?
6. Tell your three strongest points. Tell your three weakest points.
7. What is your happiest memory? (at various ages).
8. Describe the most significant event in your life.
9. Describe the characteristics of your "ideal" woman (or the "ideal" man).
10. What person besides your parents has been most influential in your life?
11. What present would you most like to receive?
12. List what your personal freedom depends upon.
13. Whose approval do you need the most?
14. In whose presence are you most uncomfortable? Why?
15. If you had what you really wanted in life, what would you have?
16. List your long-range goals. List your short-range goals.
17. Describe the most excitingly creative person you have known.
18. Write your own obituary.
19. List some creative ways to begin and to end a day.
20. What do you most daydream about?
21. What do you most trust in?
22. Who has most changed your life?
23. Where would you live if you could and what would you do there?
24. Tell who you are, apart from your titles, honors, or your job description.
25. What is the best book (apart from the Bible) you have ever read?
26. What kind of social gathering or party do you like best?
27. Describe your favourite way of spending leisure time.
28. What feelings do you have trouble expressing or controlling?
29. What kinds of things make you irritated . . . furious?
30. What makes you feel depressed or "blue"?
31. What makes you anxious, worried, or afraid?
32. What gives you self-respect?

Inter-personal (Right relationship to others)

1. Describe the person who has meant most in your life other than a parent or child. What is that person's outstanding characteristic?
2. Who was the first person you felt really understood you? What did he or she do? What was he/she like? What was his/her effect on you?
3. Are you the kind of person others confide in? Why?
4. What kind of person do you confide in?
5. What makes a person a good listener?
6. What kind of listener do you think you have been in this group?
7. How do you feel this group has listened to you both corporately and separately?
8. What makes a "good" marriage?

Responsiblity to Humankind (Right relationship to the world)

1. What would you most like to do to be remembered in history?
2. What is your ideal for the future of society (both immediate and long-range)?
3. Describe your convictions about "equality".
4. How could you help to change an injustice of which you are aware?
5. What is the greatest current need in your community? How do you think it should be handled?
6. If you were willing, what could you do to change your church? your home? your neighbourhood, your school? your job?
7. What disturbs you most about misuse of the physical resources in our world?
8. How do you personally react to the underfed and underprivileged in your country and in other areas of the world?
9. If you had limitless resources how would you use them to benefit others.

General (For use in groups or individual reflection)

1. List the things that make or keep your life complicated.
2. List the things that you do to keep your life simple.
3. List the things that you could do to make your life more simple.
4. What do you find to be the worst pressures and strains in your work?

5. What do you find most boring and unenjoyable about your work?
6. What do you enjoy most in your work?
7. What shortcomings handicap you in your work?
8. What are your special qualifications for your work?
9. How do you feel your work is appreciated by others?
10. What are your ambitions and goals in your work?
11. How do you feel about the salary or reward you get for your work?
12. How do you feel about the choice of career you have made?
13. How do you feel about the people you work with?
14. How do you feel about the way you handle money?

Items for Junior Teens

All or some of these can be used in get-acquainted games or certain ones in connection with other relationship games.
1. My name is . . .
2. I live at . . .
3. I have . . . brothers and . . . sisters.
4. I attend . . . school.
5. I am in . . . form at school this year.
6. I was born at . . .
7. The three things that I do best at school are . . .
8. The longest trip I ever took was to . . .
9. My hobby is . . .
10. My pet is . . .
11. I belong to these groups . . .
12. One of the best books I ever read was . . .
13. My favourite radio or TV programme is . . .
14. At home I help in these ways . . .
15. If I could spend one day as I please I would do these things . . .
16. The three things I want more than anything else are . . .
17. The three loveliest things I know are . . .
18. The thing I wonder about most is . . .
19. Three kinds of work I would like to do when I am grown are . . .
20. The three grown-ups I like best, next to my mother and father are . . .
21. What I like best about church is . . .
22. The things that are different which I wish we would do at church are . . .
23. What I think about the Bible . . .

Items for Older Teens

Again, these can be used in connection with a variety of games.

1. Name . . .
2. Address . . .
3. I attend . . . school.
4. School form this year . . .
5. Church I attend . . .
6. My father earns a living as . . .
7. My mother's occupation before being married (or now) . . .
8. I have lived in the following towns and states . . .
9. I take part in these activities in school, church and our town (include clubs, scouts) . . .
10. The subjects I like best in school are. . . .
11. I have these hobbies (or things I like especially to do) . . .
12. Two things I want more than anything else are . . .
13. I have read the following books and magazines recently . . .
14. The activities I've been doing this summer have been . . .
15. I have brothers (give ages) . . .
16. I have sisters (give ages) . . .
17. My jobs at home include . . .
18. Our family does these things together during the year (list some) . . .
19. The things I like best about church are . . .
20. The things I don't like about church are . . .
21. The things I wish we could do at church are . . .
22. I think my best quality is . . .
23. Probably my worst fault is . . .
24. The loveliest thing I know is . . .
25. The thing I wonder about most is . . .
26. One or two words that describe God to me are . . .

GROUP BUILDING GAMES

These are just two of the many games available for developing group awareness. They seek to help the group examine the process and the roles each individual plays. These two are non-threatening and have a fun aspect. They both should be an enjoyable experience while at the same time allowing for learning to take place.

TOWER BUILDING

Purpose:

To examine the processes of group task handling and decision-making when they are done under the pressures of time and competition.

Time:

— 5 minutes for introduction
— 20 minutes (or longer, depending on time available) to construct the tower
— period for judges to examine and report on their findings
— general discussion time — allow at least 20 to 30 minutes, depending upon the number of groups.

Materials:

Provide each group with the following materials (and nothing else):
4 pieces of thin cardboard (size of newsprint)
4 manila file folders
10 sheets of several colours of art paper size 8½ x 11
1 newspaper and 2 magazines (any size)
10 metres of string; 30 paper clips; 1 small roll of masking tape
1 small role of scotch tape; 2 pairs of scissors
1 piece of crepe coloured paper.

Procedure:

1. **Divide into groups of five.**
2. **Describe the task:** using only the materials provided, the task is to build a tower which best characterises each group.
3. **Announce the rules** for building the towers:
   a. Tower must be free-standing.
   b. Time allowed for building will be exact; a 20-minute period with a five minute warning signal, and a 30-second countdown at the end. For each second taken over the time limit, a point is deducted from the score.
   c. Constructions will be judged by outside "architectural experts" (such as the conference leader, minister, etc.).

4   Give a signal for the group to begin tower-building; and give the appropriate warning signals in due course.

5.   Have the judges, without asking questions of any members of the group, establish a rank order of the constructions on the basis of originality, creativity, use of materials, and "the message" received.

6.   In the discussion that follows, raise these questions:

    a.   How did you feel in this experience? Did you experience fulfillment or frustration? Why?

    b.   What did you learn about your own performance as a group member? Did you lead or follow? Did you dominate?

    c.   What became apparent about interaction between people in a group? How well did the group work together? Were the decisions group decisions?

An alternative set of questions are:

    a.   What decisions were made about tower design, and who made them?

    b.   What other points of decision or crisis were encountered?

    c.   Who exercised influence in each group?

    d.   Who seemed to have no influence?

    e.   How were human resources applied in each group?

    f.   To what extent were alternatives explored before undertaking a particular task?

    g.   To what extent did each group stay with a plan once adopted?

    h.   What similarities and differences in the behaviour of individual members were observed in this group in comparison with other groups?

The use of observers

This exercise can be enhanced by dividing into groups of 7 or 8 and allowing each group to appoint two as observers. (See the chapter on "Evaluating Small Groups" in Book No. 1 in this series for a description of their roles. Be sure each understands their roles.)

The observers report to their groups after the judges have presented their decisions.

Questions for group observers

1. How did the group organise for work?

2. Did one or more persons evolve into a position of leadership? Which ones? If so, what style of leadership did they use?

3. How were decisions made by this group?
   Were alternatives collected and tested?
   Did the group arrive at a consensus?
   Did one person railroad his idea through?

4. Were the personal resources of the group fully utilized?

5. Were there any clear transitions from one style to another?

6. Did you notice any "power play" by members of the group?

7. Other observations?

'MY IDEAL CHURCH' MURALS

This is a variation of the Tower Building game. The same general procedure is followed but with a different activity.

Materials for each group:

From rolls of newsprint cut two to three metres or join together large sheets of chart paper.

A selection of poster colours (buy in bottles or mix own)

Paint brushes

Textas

'Craypas' or other soft crayons

Two pair of scissors

Glue (wallpaper glue) and two brushes

4 magazines (e.g. *Women's Weekly*)

Procedure:

Each group makes a mural, using all or some of the materials provided, which symbolizes what should be included in an efficient local church to meet the needs of its members and to serve the local community. Paints or magazine clippings **must be used.** Both can be used if desired. **(Time allowed 40 to 50 minutes** with some warnings and countdown.)

The murals are fixed to the walls with masking tape

A few minutes is allowed for all to move around observing the murals

Each group appoints a 'P.R.' person who interprets the mural and then does a 'hard sell', in a light-hearted fashion, of the artistic and technical abilities of his group's mural. Audience reaction is encouraged — boos, cheers, etc.

Some form of half serious judging takes place.

Discussion following questions listed under Tower Building.

COMMUNICATION GAMES

The communication games given here are essentially concerned with developing listening skills and improve awareness of others. Each are of a non-threatening nature.

DO YOU HEAR WHAT I SAY?

Purpose: To help develop the art of listening to what the other person is really saying.

Setting: Groups of two sitting in movable chairs or on the floor at least knee level.

Time: 20 minutes or less if necessary.

Procedure:

1. **Debate:**
Each pair is to spend 10 minutes debating the subject with each taking opposite views.

Only one person can talk at a time — he must be brief and cannot be interrupted by his partner.

Before the second person can make his contribution he must first feed back what he thinks the other was saying.

The first person has the opportunity to restate his view until the second person really hears what he was saying. Then the procedure is reversed as the second person states his view. This alternates back and forth between the two.

Choose topics for discussion of which the participants will have a good general knowledge. Provide a number of alternatives from which they can choose.

Topics could include:
The family that eats together stays together.
All office blocks should have Muzak (continuous 'canned' music).
The compulsory wearing of seat belts is a good thing.
A woman's place is in the home?
Everyone should grow Australian native plants.
Sugar was truly described as 'pure, white and deadly'.
There is no need for soap powders to be advertised.

2. **Sharing of Feelings**
In a plenary session opportunity is given for sharing the feelings experienced.

3. **General Discussion:**
General discussion may follow with some feed in on the art of listening by the leader.

ECHO CIRCLES

Purpose: To improve awareness of what others are really saying. To learn that listening is an active task, not a passive one.

Setting: The groups sit in inner and outer circles with half acting as participants, half as observers.

Time: 15 to 20 minutes.

1. Start a discussion on a subject of special interest to the group.
2. After the discussion is underway, interrupt the group and tell them that before anyone speaks, he must first repeat what the previous speaker has said, to that person's satisfaction. Tell the observers to count the number of participants who give accurate accounts of what the previous speakers have said and to notice if the participants are actually listening to each other.
3. After 10 minutes, have the participants and observers exchange places and repeat the process.

Analysis   After the exercise, hold a brief discussion on how the echoing rule affected individuals.

— How did you feel?

— What did you learn about yourself as a listener?

— What is involved in active listening?

SOUNDINGS

Purpose: To experience more intense listening than often occurs.

Procedure:

Everyone assumes a comfortable position seated in a chair or on the floor.
The process is explained by the leader.

A variety of sounds are played, each followed by silence. The periods of silence lengthen as the sequence proceeds.
Each person is asked to consider each sound and silence.
— Did the sound help you recall a person of incident in your life?
— What thoughts did you have?
— Listen to the silence — what comes to your mind? What did you hear?
— What inner reactions did you have — pumping of your heart, muscular tensions?
Participants are given opportunity to comment about the listening experience without exerting any pressure for associations.

Recorded sounds:

If possible most of the following should be included:
(a) soft sounds, such as marimba, handbells, or chimes
(b) harsh sounds, such as crowd noises, motor exhaust, jack hammer
(c) low sounds, such as those produced by plucking the low strings of a piano or guitar
(d) rasping sounds, such as those of a screen being scratched
(e) high sounds, such as bird calls
(f) melodic sounds, such as that of a single guitar chord, fading away, or of a voice singing in the distance
(g) happy sounds, such as children laughing at play
(h) clanging sounds such as a string of bells
(i) monotonous sounds, such as dripping water at two different pitches, piano note being sounded

(j) pointed sounds, such as that produced by stretching paper and plastic wrap over glasses partially filled with water, then piercing the paper with a pencil

(k) rushing sounds, such as wind from a fan, or water running into a basin or toilet

(l) "hot" music, such as jazz or rock

(m) "cold" or spare music, such as the end of the first movement of Shostakovich's 10th Symphony (piccolos and bass together).

Note: In making a tape for this exercise, it may be desirable to insert a repetition of one of the sounds, such as that of children at play. The intervening silences are very important, but should not exceed one minute in length.

MISCELLANEOUS

THE CHURCH

(You will need sticky tape on hand for this game.)

1. Get together in groups of eight. Arrange your chairs so that you are facing each other — as close together as possible.

2. Give each group a sheet of paper. Explain that this sheet of paper is a symbol of the present institutional church, and everyone is to express his feelings about the institutional church to the sheet of paper in silence. Here is the procedure.

   (a) The person in each group who is holding the sheet of paper should take it and do whatever he feels about the church to the sheet of paper.

   (b) Then, without explaining what he did, this person should pass it on to the next person in the group. This person, in turn, should do what he feels and then pass it on until everyone has had a chance to express his feelings to the sheet of paper.

3. When the sheet of paper has completed its journey right around the group, the group should break the silence and start talking and sharing their feelings.

FOUR FACTS

1. On a blank sheet of paper, jot down four facts about yourself:
   - (a) My favourite game when I was a child was . . .
   - (b) My hero when I was twelve years of age was . . .
   - (c) My favourite kind of music right now is . . .
   - (d) The place I would like to live if I could live anywhere in the world is . . .

2. Of the four answers, three should be **true;** one should be a **lie.** For instance, (a) your favourite game as a child might be **hopscotch;** (b) your hero at age twelve might be **Roy Rogers;** (c) your favourite kind of music might be **classical guitar;** and (d) the place you would like to live might be the **South Sea Islands.**

3. When everyone has jotted down his four facts, get together in groups of four and let one person in each group start out by reading his four facts. Then, let the other three in the group try to guess which fact is a lie. For instance, one person might say, "I think you were lying when you said your favourite kind of music was classical guitar."
   When the three have guessed, the person should explain which answer was a lie and what was an honest answer.

4. Repeat this procedure for each person in the group of four.

9 Values Clarification Exercises

Values Clarification is not possible unless people can enter into some degree of honesty (feel they trust one another), are open to change, and are willing to explore the values dimension. Certainly the strategies are useful for other purposes (self-understanding, for instance, or developing group relationships), but this should not be considered clarification of values.

Though Values Clarification Games are very good learning experiences there are some guidelines of which you should be aware. See pages 37 and 38.

FIRE DRILL

1. Close your eyes and fantasize for a moment that your house is on fire — your family and pets are safe — and you have thirty seconds to run through your house and collect the most valuable possessions in your house as far as you are concerned.
2. In thirty seconds, jot down in particular the things that come to mind. For instance, (a) the chequebook, (b) your scrapbook, (c) fur coat, (d) antique desk, etc.
3. After thirty seconds, call time and ask everyone to get into groups of four. Let everyone explain the three most important items on the list and why. For instance, one might say, "I put down my jewellery box first because of a gold bracelet in there that belonged to my grandmother."
4. Have each person complete (and share, if desired) this sentence: "I learned I valued . . .".

MY CHILDHOOD TABLE

1. Close your eyes and think back to the years between seven and twelve in your life and try to recall the place where you ate most of your meals.
   Then on a blank sheet of paper, draw the shape of the table, such as a circle if it was round, a square if it was square, and the like.
2. Think of the various people who sat at the table during those years and represent each person at the table

with a colour, using the crayons that are available.

For instance, you might draw your father **dark blue** because he was strong and virile. Your mother might be yellow because she represented warmth and sunshine.

Include any pets or relatives who were very significant people in your childhood and any members in your family who were significantly missing, such as your dad who was away in the army.

3. Finally, think of one overall factor for the centre of your table that might represent your overall feeling about your childhood, such as **grey** if it was good and bad. If you cannot symbolize your childhood in one colour, use two or three colours, but somehow portray your feeling about your childhood with the colour in the centre of the table.

4. Get together in groups of four or eight and go around twice:

(a) The first time around, ask each person to explain his table — colours, symbols, etc.

(b) On the second time around, let everyone explain how and where this childhood table still influences his values, self-esteem, behaviour, and relationship with people today.

For instance, one person might say, "I was taught to hide my feelings, to be a man and never cry, and I still have trouble letting my feelings out — even with my wife and children."

VALUES AUCTION

Give each person $10,000 to start with (use play money or Monopoly money). Give various bonuses, so that the money levels range from about $40,000 for one person to $11,000 for one or two.

Distribute the Life Auction Catalogue sheets (see below). Ask each person to mark the four or five values they would most like to have. They should then rank those four or five in order of their importance.

Have an auction of the values. Bids must be raised by a minimum of $1,000. Record who won each value, how much was paid, and collect the money. Move the action along briskly, forcing on-the-spot decisions. Stop the auction if people run out of money.

Discuss, using such questions as these:
- Did everyone get their first choice?
- Which values were most popular? (Got most bids, cost most).
- How did the wealthier people feel? How did the poorer people feel?
- Were there any values important to the group which were not on the list? Assess the worth of these additional values in comparison to the prices fetched in the auction.
- What are the really important things in life? Are they actually things money can buy? To what degree are the most important things related to privilege or status in society?
- Look at the items which received the highest bids. Are they aspects of life most members would agree are important?

A variation is to use sealed bids: each person can spend the money available in any way (e.g. spend it all on one value, or spread it over several). Open the sealed bids and announce who has won each item, and at what cost.

Life Auction Catalogue Sheet (vary this list as you desire).

1. Artistic ability.
2. Power over things (ability to fix cars, program computers, etc.).
3. Vast wealth.
4. Physical attractiveness.
5. Ability to give love.
6. Ability to draw love from others.
7. Close and supportive family life.
8. Ability to bounce back.
9. Ability to initiate and maintain friendships.
10. Strong and growing faith.
11. Active and satisfying sex life.
12. Ability to influence others.
13. Power over other people.
14. Active and satisfying athletic life.
15. Opportunities for risk and adventure.
16. Popularity with the opposite sex.
17. A superior mind.
18. Ability to speak well in public.
19. A happy and warm marriage.
20. Activity which contributes to the good of society.
21. Musical talent.
22. Ability to think quickly and logically.

VALUE SYMBOL EXERCISE

Gather several of each of the items below OR print the list on sheets of paper, one for each group of six to eight.

dollar bill	car keys
TV guide	Bible
aspro	text book
toy gun	Australian flag.

Procedure:

1. Each group is to come to an agreement as to what each symbol represents in terms of values. For example, aspro may symbolize good health, or it may represent drug dependency. The gun may symbolize power, violence, or self-defence.

2. After each group has decided what the objects symbolize in terms of possible values, each individual in the group should arrange the objects (or write the list) according to his own hierarchy of values. The list or ranking should be from most valuable down to least valuable.

3. Individuals share their rankings with others in the group, and each group comes to an agreement as to how these objects are to be ranked.

4. Each group presents its interpretation of the symbols and its ranking to the other groups.

5. Discuss, using questions such as these:

    - Was there general agreement on what the objects symbolized?
    - How did you feel when you realized that others disagreed with you?
    - Could you agree with the group's final listing? Is there is a listing from another group which you prefer?
    - Do you think your final ordering of the objects would be acceptable to your parents? your friends? your teachers? In what ways would they differ?
    - How does your list compare with the values presented to you by your parents, or by the media, or by society at large?
    - If you could take out any two values and replace them with two of your own choosing, what values would you add?
    - Where do you think these values come from, for you?
    - Is there any particular ranking which may be called Christian?

PERSONAL COATS-OF-ARMS

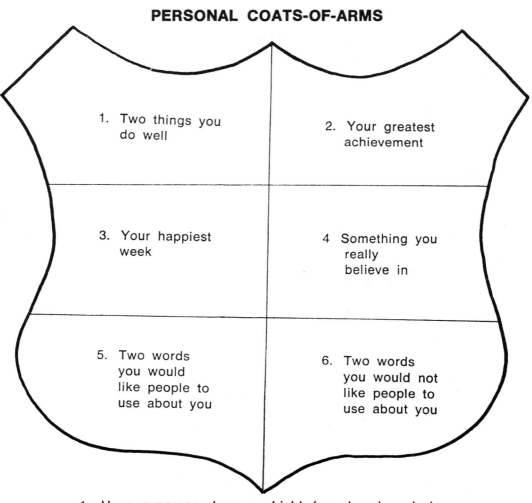

1. Two things you do well

2. Your greatest achievement

3. Your happiest week

4 Something you really believe in

5. Two words you would like people to use about you

6. Two words you would not like people to use about you

1. Have everyone draw a shield (as above) and draw something to indicate the answer in each segment.
2. Share in small groups of four.
3. Write individual statements, "I learned I value . . .".

These are a few sample exercises. For other exercises and strategies, plus values clarification, see the following books. Those marked * are basic and particularly useful.

Brian P. Hall, *Value Clarification as Learning Process*, Vol. 1, *A Guidebook for Educators.*

Brian P. Hall and M. Smith, *Value Clarification as Learning Process,* Vol. 2, *A Sourcebook for Educators.*

Brian P. Hall and M. Smith, *Value Clarification as Learning Process,* Vol. 3, *A Handbook for Christian Educators.*

M. Harmin, H. Kirschenbaum and S. Simon, *Clarifying Values through Subject Matter.* (Application for the Classroom).

Hawley and Hawley, *Human Values in the Class Room.*

Howe and Howe, *Personalised Education: Beyond Values Clarification.*

*L. Raths, M. Harmin and S. Simon, *Values and Teaching: Working with Values in the Class.*

L. Savary, *Integrating Values.*

*S. Simon, *Meeting Yourself Halfway.*

S. Simon, *I am Lovable and Capable.*

Simon et al, *Readings in Values Clarification.*

*S. Simon, L. Howe and H. Kirschenbaum, *Values Clarification: A Handbook of practical strategies for Teachers and Students.*

John H. Westerhoff, *Values for Tomorrow's Children — An Alternative Future for Education in the Church.*

10 Creative workshop programmes for building relationships

Having got this far in the preparation
These workshops aim at bringing together
the theory and methods of the two
books in this series in some practical
group building experiences.

We have devised the programmes which
follow for you to try out
with a group or to stimulate you
to create your own.

These programmes could be used one by one
at group meetings, or as the basis
for a retreat weekend.

Alternatively you may want to use only one
or two to meet the needs of a group at a
particular stage in their growth.

Some groups seem to instinctively achieve
rapport and true koinonia. Others have
reported that they grew together by slow
degrees, sometimes through pain or dissent.

We hope that these programmes may help you and
your group grow together in Christ.

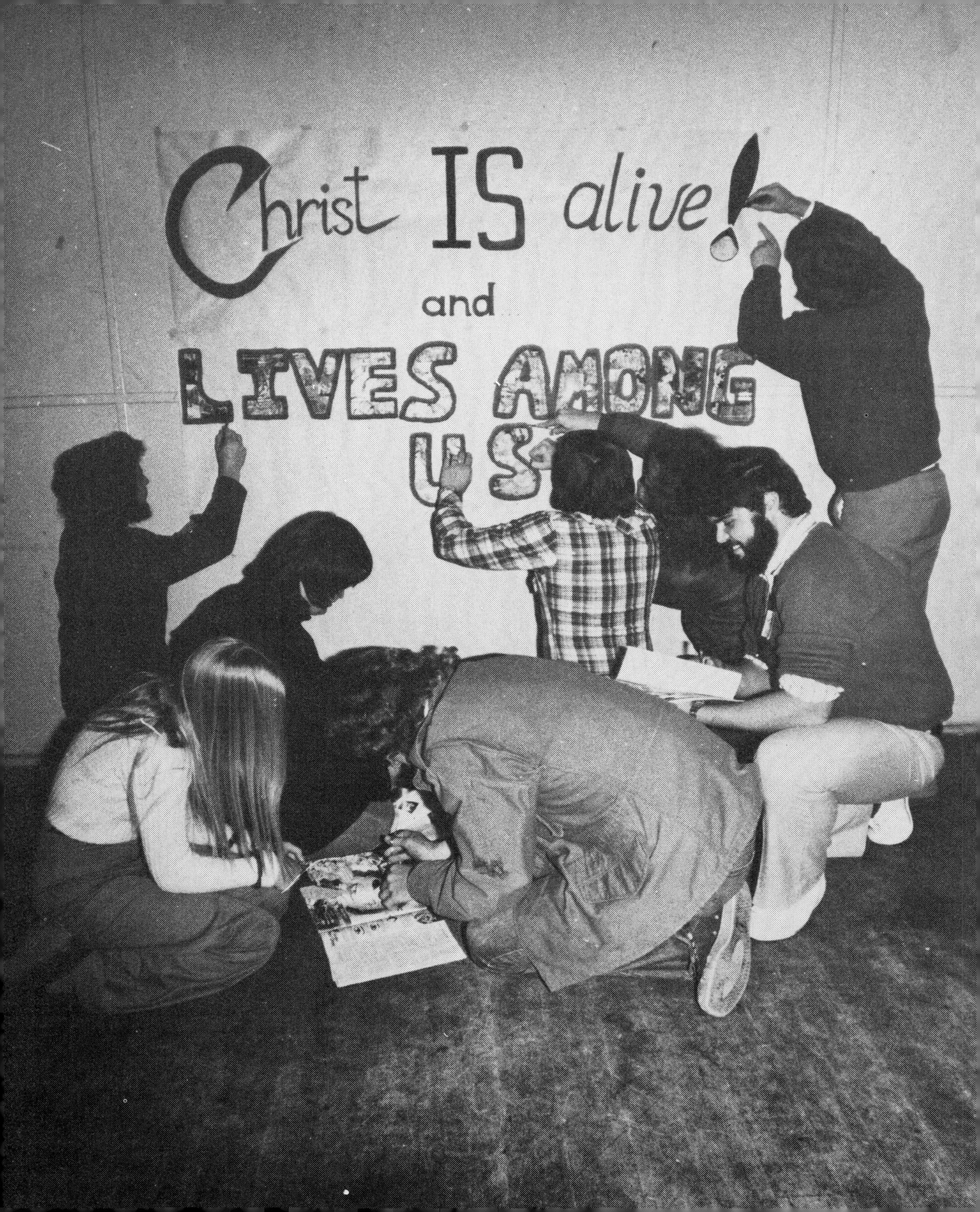
Christ IS alive!
and
LIVES AMONG
US

God is alive and living amongst us

(Dedicated to Barry)

[The title is taken from an inscribed biro purchased from Barry, a severely handicapped spastic, who sells small items from his wheelchair on the streets of Sydney. He has great difficulty in communicating verbally but has a spiritual freedom those of us who know him envy!]

PURPOSE: To stimulate faith in the divine Christ who is alive and ever present with His followers.

To show that the distinctive mark of Christian cells is their Christ-centredness and that if this is lost they may remain active by the use of good group dynamics but they will no longer be spiritually dynamic in setting people free to be part of the mighty acts of God.

COMMENT: This session has four main segments: "The Lord is Risen"; "He lives amongst us"; "He lives within us"; "Let us worship our Living Lord".

This programme is designed for at least four groups with eight to ten people in each. However, it could be effectively used by one group where only one playette is prepared.

TIME: 2 hours.

MATERIALS: Felt tip pens and cardboard for each group to create symbols; hymn books.

THE LORD IS RISEN

(45 minutes)

Brief discussion: What was the state of mind of the disciples after the crucifixion? What hopes for the future do you think they had?

Playettes: Read the following passages — Luke 24:1-12; John 20:1-10; 19-23; John 21:1-14.

Let different groups be responsible for preparing and presenting playettes, mimes or play reading using a narrator and other readers for the spoken words, based on the four scripture passages.

Discussion in groups or in a plenary session: What was the state of mind of the disciples after it was established that Jesus was alive?

How did the certainty of His risen presence sharing with them influence their behaviour?

HE LIVES AMONGST US

(20 minutes)

Read Matthew 28:20 — now refer to its immediate context, for the promise carries with it obligations.

General Discussion: Can you think of ways in which such a promise should bring serenity, hope, courage, strength?

Can you recall a time when you have experienced this in your own life?

What could it mean for our group life if we took this seriously? How would it affect — our relationships
                     — our worship
                     — our study
                     — our concern for each other
                     — our concern for others.

HE LIVES WITHIN US

(40 minutes)

Bible Encounter: Apply Professor Ross Snyder's Bible Study Method (abbreviated version), Segments A, B, C—(a and b), on pp. 79, 80.

LET US WORSHIP OUR LIVING LORD

(15 minutes)

[Begin by selecting one or two hymns which sum up the theme of this session.]

He is here: Read Matthew 18:20 and make a simple symbol in no more than two minutes and place in the centre of the group to symbolise His presence.

Spend a few minutes in **silent meditation** reflecting on what it meant for the early disciples and the Christian Church down through history for Christ to be amongst them.

Let as many as wish to respond in one sentence prayers.

Let Us Praise Him: Sing the hymns selected.

We hear the Word of Our Living God: Read in unison or responsively Psalm 139: 1-10, 17, 18.

Let Us Respond in Prayer: If time permits let each write a brief prayer in response to the whole session which is then read by each in turn, or ask for one sentence, spontaneous verbal prayers.

Pass the Peace: Around the group in turn or at random, each takes the hand of another and says "The Lord is alive and living among us". The other responds "He is indeed alive, praise His Name". Alternatively conclude by standing in a close circle around the symbol of Christ's presence, arms around each other, and recite the above words together as a group.

Trust me!

PURPOSE: To develop awareness of what is involved in trust relationships between people and trust in God.

TIME: 1½ to 2 hours.

MATERIALS NEEDED: Blindfolds, board for "Jet Trip", chart paper, felt tip pens, craypas, paints, coloured paper, masking tape.

TRUST IN HUMAN RELATIONSHIPS

(30 minutes)

Cartoons: Display cartoon No. 1 and allow a light-hearted discussion centred around why the man looks so happy about jumping over a cliff which has rocks and hard ground at its base!

Display cartoon No. 2. Discuss — What word could describe the man's relationship to those below? You may want to list these but it isn't essential. The word "Trust" usually emerges — if not, suggest it in the discussion.

Trust "Games": Use **one** of the following "games". Follow either with the period of discussion and sharing.

Trust Walk. Divide the group into pairs. Have one partner blindfold the other. If meeting in a home, plan a course for the game using a number of rooms and hallway. Move all the unbreakable (!) furniture around in the rooms and distribute chairs about the hall. The blindfolded person negotiates the course by themselves without any help from their partner. (When an outdoor or hall situation is available, set up a number of suitable obstacles — chairs, tables, boxes, old tyres, etc.) Explain that the obstacles must not be pushed out of the way but gone around or over. When all have completed the course then it is again negotiated with the aid of the "seeing" partner. Repeat with the other partner going through the same experience.

In an outdoor experience the first solo walk can be eliminated and a longer guided walk used.

This can be varied in a situation with plenty of room by working in teams of six or eight. Line up with both hands on the shoulders of the person in front. All but the lead person are blindfolded.

Jet Trip: Send a number of people out of the room. They are brought back one at a time, blindfolded. Have them remove their shoes with the explanation that this will reduce the risk of them breaking their ankles! The person then boards their single seater jet which will malfunction soon after take-off, requiring them to eject.

However . . . they forgot to put on a parachute! But . . . never fear, the squadron leader will rush out to catch them. The jet — a plank or sturdy piece of board — should be at least 1½ metres long and 1/3 of a metre wide, is held by two strong group members. The pilot mounts the plank and to steady themselves may place one hand on the shoulder of a tall person who stands close to the plank. This tall person should gradually and slowly lower himself while the board is lifted no more than a few centimetres off the floor.

The onlookers all add their encouragement and warnings about the approaching ceiling (and any other spontaneous remarks!). The leader announces the malfunction of the aircraft and directs the pilot to eject by jumping off the plank to the floor with the assurance that squadron leader "Muscles" will be there to catch him or her. Repeat until all those outside the room have participated.

Plenary Discussion and Sharing:

How did you feel?
What did you learn about trust?
What does it involve?
(List learnings about trust on a chart.)

TRUST STATEMENTS

(25 minutes)

Individual Work. Each read the resource sheet at the end of this session outline "Developing Trust Relationships" and underline the most significant aspects.

Plenary. What additional things did you learn about trust? Add feedback to chart used at end of Trust Games.

Divide into groups of 6 or 8.

Formulate a statement together which defines trust and reflects the experiences and learnings so far in this session. The dictionary definitions of trust at the end of the session outline should be referred to.
The statement is printed onto a chart.

Plenary. A person from each group holds up the chart and reads their statement. Each chart is then fixed to the wall or placed on the floor in the centre of the groups.

TRUST'S HIGHEST OBJECT — GOD

(30-40 minutes)

Bible Research. In small groups read the following scripture passages. (Where a number of small groups are involved assign one or two passages to each. If there is only one group select three or four passages.)

Psalm 35:5, Psalm 5:11, Psalm 32:10, Psalm 118:8, Proverbs 3:5, Isaiah 26:3, 1 Timothy 6:17, Hebrews 11:6.

Discuss: What do these teach us about trust in God? What does trust involve?

Plenary: List the small group findings on a chart.

Bible Paraphrase. (As an alternative to the Bible Research.) "Commit your way to the Lord; trust in Him, and he will act." (Psalm 37:5)

As a group make a paraphrase of this verse. Take each word and decide upon its meaning first. (Use a dictionary.) Keep it simple. Write it so someone with little or no church background could understand it.

Sharing (to follow the alternative segments above) either in small groups or in a plenary session. Can you think of a situation in which you really did trust God?
or
Use the Desert Pete meditation at the end of this session outline.

CREATE A WALL MURAL

In small groups make a mural using words, symbols and pictures to gather the most significant learnings from this session and the action which the group feels it should take individually and/or collectively.

Developing trust relationships

We need each other. No person is an island — we live in community. We are gregarious beings who normally socialise, relating to each other in many ways — good or bad, helpful or unhelpful. A healthy human relationship of any depth has trust as one of its main ingredients. If we can't trust others, meaningful relationships which bring the best out in each other will never develop to any worthwhile degree.

We cannot begin to trust other people, we cannot begin to risk mistakes, until we have begun to trust ourselves.

Trust, in the sense we are using it, means this ability to risk yourself, to put yourself in the hands of another, to put yourself at the service of another. And you just do not do that until you own yourself, that is, until you have enough self-confidence and self-possession that you can afford to "let yourself go". Trust is always a risk, a kind of leap in the dark. It is not based on any solid proof that the other person will not hurt you. If you have that kind of proof, you are dealing with a sure thing, and trust is always a gamble. That's why the capacity to trust comes from inside, not outside. The "sure thing" is your own worth, your own certainty in yourself, not the certainty you have in another. That comes later — after you've trusted someone and he has not let you down.

We are not dealing at this point with the kind of trust a child has in his parents or the trust a religious person places in his God. Such trust is based on the manifest goodness or trustworthiness of the person trusted; it is evoked from without. The capacity to trust that we are concerned with here is an inner quality of emotional maturity and it affects all human relationships, not just specialized ones.

To trust, then, is to take the initiative, to make the first step towards another, to hold out your hand, to say "I like you" before you are sure what the other person will say in return. This naturally leads to the question: How does a person go about gaining the kind of self-confidence that enables him to trust others? From others. Other people have to convince us that we are lovable, acceptable, and significant. Initially that's the essential job of parents. It is the role of friends. And it should be the role of educators, too.

Family, friends and teachers are primary sources of a person's self-image. These sources broaden as life progresses. If that combination of influence helps a person discover his own worth, he in turn will be in a position to trust others, to go out to them and in the process help others discover their own worth. That seems to be what human relations are all about — helping each other respect ourselves to the point where we can afford to give of ourselves to others.

Nobody is going to discover his or her own worth over night. That is a long process; but at least it is possible to help people realise the importance of being able to trust others and to realise that it depends on how they regard themselves.

Trust, like respect, is basic to human relationships. Trust goes one step further than respect. To respect someone is to honour him or her as a human being, to assume that he or she is basically good in intention and action. To trust someone is to get involved, to act out of your respect, to risk yourself to some degree. So if respect is the foundation of human relationships, trust is the relationship itself. We should become aware of our own ability or inability to trust.

Trust involves responsibility and commitment. When someone trusts us with their confidence in a variety of ways, we accept an obligation to justify that person's trust in us.

Every time a person's trust in another is betrayed, they find it more difficult to enter into a future trust relationship. Unfortunately, some have been betrayed so frequently that they have lost much of their own confidence in themselves and in their ability to assess other people as worthy of their trust. They usually also develop an unwillingness to make further ventures in trust.

You cannot force a person to trust any more than you can force a person to recognize his own worth.

We all have self-confidence to a degree — the more we have the better — and we keep growing in it all our lives. The same is true of our ability to trust.

Trust — some dictionary definitions

— A firm belief in the honesty, truthfulness, justice or power of a person or thing.
— An obligation or responsibility imposed on one in whom confidence or authority is placed.
— Have confidence or faith in . . .
— To rely on or depend on . . .

DESERT PETE MEDITATION

1. **In silence** each person reads the meditation and relates it to himself or herself personally. Ask yourself this question. "What does this mean to **me**"? Be honest with yourself.
2. Let each person share with the rest of the group what the Meditation meant to them personally.

The Meditation

A man was lost in the desert. He stumbled along, his throat parched, his lips cracked. Then there before him was an old water pump. He used his remaining strength to grasp the handle and pump furiously. No water came. In despair, he sat down, too tired and too thirsty to go on. Suddenly he saw an old rusty tin can in front of him, in it was a piece of paper carefully wrapped. He unwrapped the paper and found this note. "Thus pump has a leather washer. The washer must be wet for the pump to work. Under the big board there is a small bottle of water; just enough to prime the pump. If you drink any of it there won't be enough to wet the washer. If you pour it all on the washer, you will have water to spare." Signed . . . Desert Pete.

From *Dare to Live Now* by Larson

What will I do with my life — my bottle of water? I can use it all for short term purposes and it will be gone, or I can use it to "prime the pump" and get, not only everlasting life but the fullness of life that Jesus offers to us each day.

In order to prime the pump, I must have faith; faith to put my life in the hands of Jesus Christ. Faith to say, "Lord, do with me as you will".

How much faith do I have? Do I have the faith to follow Desert Pete's advice? Do I have faith enough to put my life totally in Jesus' care and at his disposal?

Hear ye!
Hear ye!

PURPOSE: To help develop skills in listening.

RESOURCES: "Building Small Groups"

Chapter 9 "Keeping Group Life Vital"

**MATERIALS
NEEDED:**   Pencils, writing pads.

1. Listening to the sounds in our environment

Preliminary exercise: Each person, taking a pencil and writing pad, goes outside the building, ideally into a garden or bushland setting. Keeping a strict rule of silence and endeavouring to be unaware of others near them, they individually list all of the sounds they hear.

(If the venue does not permit the above activity substitute the listening game "Soundings" using a pre-recorded tape, found on page 190 of this book.

Or — with each person working individually play a record of a movement of a symphony such as the storm in Beethoven's "Pastoral" Symphony; or Fingal's "Cave Overture" (Mendelssohn); or Rick Wakeman's "Jane Seymour" from "The Six Wives of Henry VIII"; or Sibelius' Violin Concerto in D Minor"; or his "The Swan of Tuonela"; or "Venus" or other movements from Holst's "The Planets" or similar music with sustained themes, which will evoke a mood, a reaction. Each person listens letting their imagination run riot and then note down what they heard beyond the sounds of the orchestra — what situation did it help them recall or what did they fantasize as the music played (e.g. a gathering storm, busy traffic, waves on the sea shore, children playing or a peaceful scene from a mountain look-out at sunset).

Sharing: (10 mins.) Each is given opportunity to share their experience, the sounds they heard, their fantasies and their feelings. (Where a large number are involved, cluster in groups of 6 or 8.) What did you learn? — about our environment; about listening; about life itself.

2. Listening to each other

(20 mins — add 15 mins if optional segment included)

Individually read "Some Communication Skills . . . 1. Paraphrasing" in Chapter 9, "Building Small Groups".
Use one of the listening games, such as "Do you hear what I say" found on page 188 of this book.
(Optional) **Individually** read "How to Listen to Others" on page 132 in Chapter 9 in "Building Small Groups". Underline which is personally most helpful. Share findings with those immediately involved in this exercise.

3. Listening to the Voice of God

(40 to 60 mins)

Use the Meditative use of the Bible Method found on pages 97 to 99 and follow with the Dialogue Prayer Method on pages 154-155.

Where to from here?

In a plenary segment share:
What were the most significant experiences you had?
What do you hope to do as a result of this experience?

Affirmation workshops

PURPOSE: To identify our own strengths and hear from the group how these match up with what they see to be our strengths.

To learn something of the ministry of affirmation by exercising it in the group and exploring together some relevant Bible passages and a resource.

HOW TO USE THIS MATERIAL: The material falls into **three** major sections:

— Resource — "The Ministry of Affirmation"

— Affirmation experiences

— Bible encounters.

Each affirmation workshop will include these three segments:

— Select one affirmation experience from the four alternatives given
  • Strength Bombardments
  • Sandwich-board Messages
  • Bags-a-tell
  • Art Gallery.

— Use the resource "The Ministry of Affirmation" by each individually reading and underlining significant and helpful points, then each shares these with the rest of the group.
    (Allow 20 to 25 minutes)

— Select one of the Bible encounters from the three provided.
  • Love Builds Us
  • Ministering To Each Other
  • Fulfilling a Barnabas Role.

THE MINISTRY OF AFFIRMATION

Affirmation is one of the ways Christians help each other to become. Its purpose is to enable the awareness and acceptance of these distinctive positive strengths which God has given to each individual for the enrichment of the Christian fellowship and the world in general. When we bless each other in this way there can result growth in self awareness and acceptance by individuals of their own distinctive and unique positive characteristics which result in their special contribution to the Body of Christ.

Most feedback from the world is negative and self destructive. Authority figures — parents, teachers, leaders, superiors and some peers — put so much effort into telling us we are no good that most of us are convinced and act accordingly. Too much Christian fellowship is characterised by its fault finding, condemnation, criticism and rebuke. Jesus said, "I came that you may have life and have it abundantly." Many disciples give the impression that Jesus was mistaken — that really His purpose was to crush people rather than set them free to know abundant life.

The crux of Christianity is a vital personal encounter with the living Christ. "If anyone is in Christ he is a new creation; the past is finished and gone, everything has become fresh and new. Christian discipleship is allowing God in Christ to set us free and daily live out His life through us rather than allowing ourselves to be forced into moulds the shape of other people's brand of Christianity.

The church is suffering from a shortage of Barnabases ("the son of encouragement") to exercise the ministry of encouragement a little more frequently than the ministry of rebuke.

Pride is one of the greatest curses most of us have to contend with. Unfortunately some have been so preoccupied with helping others keep humble that many a Christian trudges along with unreal guilt and a sense of inferiority, like a convict's ball and chain, fixed to their ankle restricting them from really going somewhere for God. People who over-exercise the ministry of rebuke are often projecting their own problems.

If we are able to accept God's acceptance of us in Christ and accept ourselves as we are in this state of becoming then we will be more likely to "love as He loved" and sincerely affirm the strength of others. For that is what *"agape"* love is all about — seeking the good of others, always supporting, caring, building up in love.

The ministry of affirmation involves sincerity and honesty. It does not affirm what is not there, although it may recognise what is only beginning to emerge in a person. It may fan a tiny spark into a flame. But it never flatters or butters people up. That false affirmation is not of the Spirit, it is usually self-seeking, hindering rather than enabling.

To experience genuine affirmation can be an exodus experience — releasing from the bondage of a negative and destructive past, to God's promised land of freedom, challenge, growth and ministry.

Rather than making one proud, it can lead to the emergence of a warm humility which grows out of gratitude to the one from whom these strengths originated. It will be a humility born of love within rather than the bitter fruit of others working off their own hang-ups on us.

Affirming the strengths of others may or may not be a recognition of the spiritual "gifts" which God has given to each believer for the building up of the body. I draw a distinction here for it is no light thing to discern the special spiritual abilities which the Holy Spirit bestows. However, to encourage, to help people become aware of who they are and the unique person God made them may be for some the first step to recognition of the "gifts of the Spirit" to which Paul refers in his epistles.

Our prime calling as Christians is to set people free — not to impose new burdens, to help them do their duty or make them good. Our role is that of spiritual midwives helping to enable the elimination of the perverted pseudo-Christianity of "oughtness" (law) and replacement of it with a birth of being and doing and excitement and wonder and newness which grows out of the freedom Christ alone can give (grace).

STRENGTH BOMBARDMENTS

Time: Can take up to 1½ hours for groups of 8-10.

Materials: Large sheet of chart paper and a felt tip pen for each person; masking tape.

Individual work: Each person is given a sheet of chart paper which is folded lengthwise. On one side each writes down what they consider to be their strengths. At the top of the other side the person writes their name.

Group Work: Each person in turn fixes their sheet to the wall or a chart board with the blank side out bearing their name. Members of the group affirm the person by writing on the blank sheet one word which describes a strength of that person. They put their name or initials after each word. Brief comments are made by the person doing the affirming when necessary. When the listing is complete the leader asks of the person affirmed, "How do you feel about the total list?" "Anything very special to you on that list?" "Any surprises?"

The person then opens up the chart, re-fixing it so both lists are visible. A brief comparison between both lists is done by both that person and the leader.

After all have presented their charts time should be spent in locating the things which block these strengths and how to remove these blocks.

(N.B. The words we give to others in this exercise tell us a lot about ourselves — they may be a commentary on ourselves.)

Affirmation experience

SANDWICH BOARD MESSAGES

Time: 30 to 45 minutes for a group of 8 to 10.

Materials Needed: Two large pieces of cardboard approximately one metre by 2/3 metre (cut from used large cardboard boxes), two sheets of chart paper similar size to the cardboard, string and a felt tip pen for each person and masking tape.

Preparation: Link the cardboard together to form a sandwich board to fit over a person's head using pieces of string. Fix the paper to the boards with masking tape.

Individual Work: Each person writes on one board single words which describe how they see themselves — who they are; their strengths, etc.

Group Work: Each person puts on their sandwich board with the blank board to the back. The group move around reading each other's boards and then writing one word on the back which describes that person's strengths.

Group Sharing: This is followed by a sharing time using similar questions to each person as those in "Strength Bombardments".

Affirmation experience

BAGS-A-TELL

Time: 45 to 60 minutes for a group of 10.

Materials Needed: A large self-standing paper bag (from food supermarket), a magazine (such as a Women's Weekly), a pair of scissors, a saucer of paste (made from flour and water or wall paper glue), small glue brush and a felt tip pen for each person.

Individual Work: (Approx. 15 minutes) Each person writes their name on the top of their bag on both sides. (The felt tip pens are not used for the rest of the exercise.) Each then goes through their magazine cutting out words and pictures which describe who they are and where they are at. These are then glued to the outside of the bag.

Group Work: The bags are then placed self standing in a row so the names are clearly displayed. Each person then goes through their magazine again looking for words or pictures which describe the strengths of others. These are cut out and placed inside the appropriate bags after first signing their name on it and writing any appropriate comment on it if it is necessary (e.g. on a picture of a bridge one may write, "I see you as one who helps bridge gaps between people"; on a picture of a lightglobe one may write "You have deep insights which bring helpful light to our discussions". Each tries to find at least one for each person in the group, limiting to 2 or 3 what they put in any one bag.

Group Sharing: Each person in turn explains what they meant to convey on the outside of the bag. They then take the clippings from the inside of the bag, hold them up for all to see and reading them out. The leader asks, "How do you feel about our gifts to you?" "Can you accept them as our sincere affirmation of who you are?" "What was a new learning for you?" "Which especially encourages you?"

Variation: Cardboard boxes with the tops left open can be used instead of the paper bags.

Affirmation experience

ART GALLERY

Time: 45 to 60 minutes.

Materials Needed: 1 piece of large chartpaper, a magazine (such as Women's Weekly), paste, scissors, brush and masking tape for each person.

Individual Work: Each person writes their name on the top of their sheet of paper and fixes it to the wall using masking tape. Each turns through their magazine selecting words or pictures which indicate the strengths of various group members. These are glued to the appropriate sheets on the wall.

Group Sharing: One sheet is taken at a time with group members saying why they chose what they fixed to the person's chart.
Similar questions to those given in the preceding exercises are directed to the person concerned.

Variations: In homes where it may not be appropriate to fix the charts to the wall use large cardboard boxes — one side for each person's chart.
Instead of using magazine cuttings, each draws symbols or writes words on the charts (this considerably shortens the time for the exercise).

ALTERNATIVE BIBLE STUDIES

1. **Love Builds Us**

   Apply Professor Ross Snyder's Depth and Encounter Bible Study Method (abbreviated form if restricted in time on pages 81-83) to John 13:34, 35.

2. **Ministering to each other.**

   Individually read Peter 1 4:8-11, Corinthians Ch. 12 and Romans 12:4-8 underlining, or writing on a separate sheet, words or phrases which describe the ministry which every Christian disciple is called to exercise.

   — What do we learn from this about ministry within the Christian fellowship?

   — What do you personally find most helpful?

   — What action should you be taking as a result of this learning?

   — How can we enable each other in the taking of this action?

   Group Sharing: Each shares response to first question. This can be recorded on a chart.

   Each individually reads and underlines significant points in the first three paragraphs on page 11 of Book No. 1 "Building Small Groups" (or the leader or a participant can present a chart summary of the main points) which is then compared with the group's findings for the first question.

   Each shares their personal response to the other three questions.

3. **Fulfilling a Barnabas Role** (or being 'Sons of Encouragement')

   As a group, using a concordance and a number of commentaries, do research into the life and ministry of Barnabas in the Book of Acts noting his personal characteristics and the ways in which he exercised his ministry of encouragement. Note findings on charts. Let each **individually** reflect on the group findings and seek to apply it to their own lives by responding to:—

If I took Barnabas as a model for my life and ministry in what specific ways would change be needed?
What aspects of his life and ministry do I already have to some degree?

Each shares their response to these questions with the group giving any necessary further affirmation to each person's feedback on the second question.

If I have all the eloquence
   of men or of angels,
but speak without love,
      I am simply a gong booming
      or a cymbal clashing....

Love is always patient and kind;
   it is never jealous;
   Love is never boastful or conceited;
   it is never rude or selfish;
   it does not take offence,
   and is not resentful.

Love takes no pleasure in
   other people's sins
   but delights in the truth;
   it is always ready to excuse,
   to trust, to hope,
   and to endure whatever comes.

Love does not come to an end.

. . . 1 Corinthians 13:1-7
(Jerusalem Bible)

The greatest force in the world . . .

PURPOSE: To present 'agape' love is the distinctive factor in Christian fellowship which is the life of God in Christ.
To seek to experience something of this love together and extend it to others who are not easy to love.

TIME: 1½ to 2 hours.

MATERIALS NEEDED: Ruled file cards approximately 15 x 8 cm for each person.

FROGHOOD

(30 to 40 mins)

— Read "Kiss a Frog" on page 6.

— Prepare and Present a Role Play or playette based on "Kiss a Frog".

— Discuss the issues raised in the role play. What are the characteristics of a human frog? What is really involved in 'frog kissing'?

— Share one aspect of your life which God has touched with His love and brought about changes.

— Individually write on the piece of card supplied an anonymous description of a person who is a "frog" to you, e.g. a person at work, a relative, etc. Write this on the top line of the card, keeping this to one line.

'LOVE, LOVE, LOVE'

(40-50 mins)

— Use the Silent Sharing Bible Study Method found on page 115 with 1 Corinthians 13:1-7.

— As a group take each aspect of love in 1 Corinthians 13:1-7 and discuss how each could affect our relationship to each other in the group. What does each aspect involve? When have we seen this love amongst us? How would our group change if this love was always present?

COVENANTS TO HELP FROGS GET KISSED

(15-20 mins)

Each person in the group passes the card, on which they wrote the anonymous description of a person who is a "frog" to them, to the person on their left. That person repeats on the card what they had written on their own card. The cards are passed around and written on until each receives back their own card which will contain the descriptions of every other group member's "frog".

In silence let each individual write out a positive one sentence prayer on the reverse side of the card for their own "frog" and a general one sentence prayer covenanting to pray for the problem persons of other group members for the next seven days.

Let the group hold hands around the circle symbolic of their covenant together to support each other in prayer outside the group. Any number can pray verbally responding to the whole session.

Conclude with an appropriate scripture chorus or hymn.

People matter . . .

PURPOSE: To enable an understanding of some of the more negative roles people play in small groups and how to help these people.
To give some help in the development of good interpersonal relationships in Christian groups.

TIME: 1½ to 2 hours.

MATERIALS NEEDED: Large name-tags for characters in role plays.

RESOURCE: "Building Small Groups" Chapter 7.
"Understanding and Helping Group Members."

THE PEOPLE WE MEET IN SMALL GROUPS

(30 to 55 mins)

The Procedure: Two people are assigned to each character. The first person should act and talk exactly as the person in the situation would act and talk. The second person will be the "alter ego". He should say and do what the character is thinking and feeling inside. The "alter ego" can speak at any time in the role play, leaning over the shoulder of the character with which they are aligned.

The characters will be drawn from Chapter 7 "Understanding and Helping Members of Small Groups" — "Helping Problem Members" in "Building Small Groups".

The principal characters arrange their chairs in a semi-circle facing each other. The "alter egos" stand immediately behind the person they represent.

One or two observers may be used to sit facing the principal characters. They do not join in the drama but observe carefully the roles played by both the main characters and their "alter egos". In a large group, the balance of the participants will all play the role of observers.

ROLE PLAY 1

(10-15 mins)

Chief Characters: Marty Luther, Chattering Charlie, Silent Sam, Negative Norm and Peaceful Paul. All read the descriptions of these problem people in Chapter 7. (**Do not read** the suggestions for helping them.)

Assign Roles. Main characters (being sure to avoid placing people in their natural roles!), alter egos, and observers.

Situation: The stately old St. Agatha's Church in Conservativeville is not well known for innovative programmes. Sunday morning worship is fairly well attended as evidenced by the 100 or so late model cars on the church's large parking lot adjacent to the church. A number of more progressive recent appointees to the church council have been responsible for the calling of their first minister under 40, since the church was established 89 years ago.

More thoughtful people, both young and old, have been complaining about the lack of life in the gathering worship of the church. The new minister, well known as a thoughtful innovator, has introduced some new forms of worship during his first 12 months. The seating has been re-arranged, a youth musical group participates occasionally, laymen lead a large proportion of all services and forms of service are used to involve the congregation. Most are pleased with the more creative worship but Marty Luther is concerned and has invited some of the more senior members of the church council to his home to discuss the new direction of the church life.

Description of Chief Characters

Marty Luther is in his early 60s. He has been a lay preacher (or catechist) for 35 years. His grandfather, an ordained minister, held the highest position in the national courts of his denomination. Marty is very conservative and longs for the "good old days" when the "house full" notice needed to be placed outside St. Agatha's Church.

Chattering Charlie likes the new minister and thinks he should be given a fair go. He hasn't been in the church as long as the others but has become deeply involved.

Peaceful Paul is 55 next birthday. He is a tradesman and highly respected by all. He has a genuine concern for people.

Negative Norm owns a small family business which hasn't changed much over the last 60 years. He doesn't have much time for the ordained ministry, especially if they don't see things his way.

Timing: Allow about 3 to 5 minutes for the role play with additional time for preparation, i.e. explanation of procedures, roles and setting.

FISH BOWLING

(20 to 40 mins)

All involved in the drama sit in a circle leaving one vacant chair. If there are more than the two observers, have them form an outer circle, otherwise have the two observers stand outside the inner circle. The inner circle discusses the issues and when a person on the outside circle wishes to join in the discussion the spare chair is taken for the period of his contribution . . . It is then vacated by him. The inner circle exchanges places with an equal number from the outer circle when the leader feels it will facilitate the discussion, or at about halfway through the time allocated.

What can we learn about human behaviour in small groups from this drama?

Taking each of the chief characters in turn discuss how you would help them contribute positively in a small group.

(During this discussion some in the outer group will read up the suggested ways of helping them in Chapter 9 and contribute this as a proposal if needed.)

ROLE PLAY 2

(10-15 mins)

(This may be used as an option to No. 1 or in addition to it, if time permits.)

Adopt the same procedure for this role play.

Situation: Blue Hills High School Parents and Citizens Association have run very successful fetes each year, however last year's was a flop. At their last meeting they appointed a small sub-committee to explore ways of ensuring the success of the next fete. The committee is meeting in Dorothy's home unit.

Chief Characters: Domineering Dorothy has been president for the last 15 years. She isn't open to suggestions. She is manager/owner of a very successful women's clothing shop. Her family are now all at University or in various professions but she still maintains her interest in (and hold over!!) the P. & C.

I-Irene is a very capable person (and is well aware of it!). She has plenty of good ideas. The fete sub-committee is chaired by her.

Prickle Pete. Pete runs his own building contracting business. He is at the meeting because his wife has "dobbed" him in to erect the stalls. He isn't really very happy about being there!

But Bill. Bill has been a hard worker at every fete for the last 8 years. He does whatever he is asked to do without complaining.

GUIDELINES FOR RELATIONSHIPS

(60 minutes)

Apply the **Silent Sharing Method** (20-30 min.) found on page 115 to one of the following passages:

Philippians 2:1-8
Romans 12:3-21
Ephesians 4:15-32
1 John 3:11-18; 4:13-21

General Discussion (15 min.) follows the completion of the above method, centred on the following.
What principles or guidelines for helping relationships in groups can we draw from this passage? Make a list.

COMPILE AN EPISTLE

As a group compile an "Epistle to Leaders and Members of Small Groups" (20 min.). Draw together the learnings from this session by imagining you are a group of apostles compiling a letter to a new Christian group which has just been formed in a distant city.

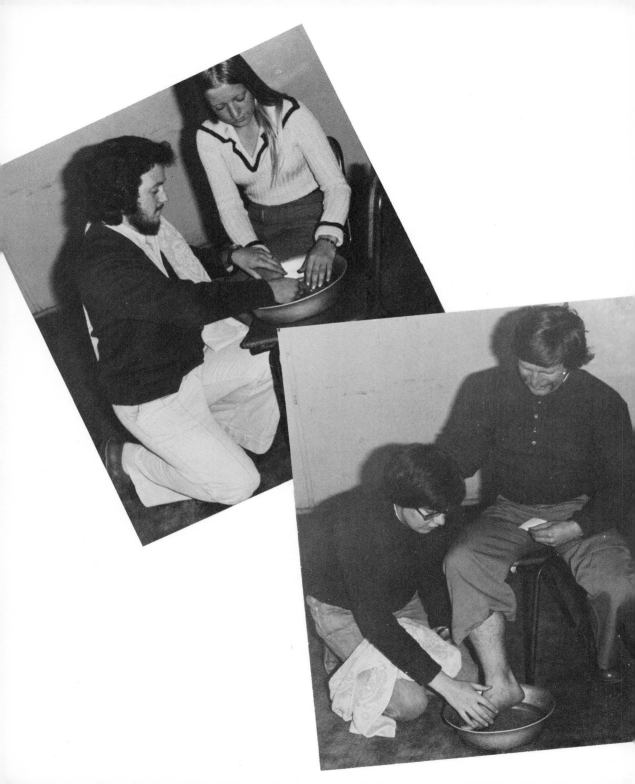

The fellowship
of the
bowl and towel

PURPOSE: To gain inspiration and motivation from Christ's life of servanthood in order to enrich personal lifestyle and Christian community.

TIME: 1½ to 2 hours.

MATERIALS NEEDED: Filmstrip, slides or wallcharts, towels and bowls. Chartpaper, felt tipped pens and craypas.

1. JESUS' EXAMPLE OF HUMILITY AND SERVANTHOOD

(60 mins)

JESUS WASHES THE DISCIPLES' FEET

John 13:1-17. Use a film strip which is based on this passage. If this is not available use suitable frames from other filmstrips or slides or large wall posters, with three people reading the passage — narrator, Jesus, Peter.

Role Play (in Groups of 10-12) 15-20 min.
Let the group endeavour to catch something of the majesty and moving humility of this very significant event as the Creator knelt at the feet of the created as their servant Lord. (The spirit will be lost if it cannot be performed with solemnity.) Half the group should take a bowl and towel each and wash the feet of the remainder. Allow individuals to select their roles. Some will prefer to be involved as observers — this can be equally moving. Don't coerce any to be involved.

Some alternatives. Do the foot-washing in a symbolic manner without using water but with empty bowls and towels. **Or** wash each others hands, possibly with the person doing the washing kneeling on the floor.

Sharing. Let the group share the feelings they had during the role playing.

THE DISCIPLES' REACTION

(20 min.)

Before suggesting the reaction of the disciples to their feet-washing recall something of their diversity of character.

Peter
— A born leader and the natural spokesman of the group. (John 6:68; 21:3; Matthew 16:16).
— Gallant, generous hearted, affectionate, impetuous.
— With defects — often too outspoken (Matthew 16:23; 19:27) — disowned Christ (Matthew 26:69ff).

Andrew
— His name in Greek means brave, or manly.
— Continually eclipsed by his brother Simon Peter.
— As a young man deeply stirred by John the Baptist's revival movement (John Chapter 1).
— Always busy introducing someone to Jesus (John 1:42, 6:8f; 12:20-22).

John
— Had perfectly united manly strength and womanly tenderness.
— Faithful to the last (John 19:26).
— Meditative, thoughtful, prayerful.
— But with a less pleasing side (Mark 9:38; Luke 9:54; Mark 10:35ff).
— Passionate love for Jesus.

Judas Iscariot
— Jesus must have seen in him at one time the makings of a real apostle.
— Originally attracted and fascinated by Jesus (political motivation?) — left all to follow Jesus.
— Now with a disillusioned, bitter and vengeful spirit.

Simon, the Zealot
— The fiery nationalist.

(These notes are derived from P.61ff of *The Life and Teaching of Jesus Christ* by James S. Stewart published by Church of Scotland Committee on Youth 1965 — a book well worth having on your bookshelves.)

Group Discussion. Take each of the above disciples one by one and attempt to assess the feeling they would have, in the light of their respective characters, to the washing of their feet by the Lord. (N.B. Peter's reaction in Vs. 6-11— What feeling was he expressing?)

JESUS' MOTIVATION

(15 min.)

Why did Jesus minister to his disciples in this way?

Individually underline the reason which seems most likely,

then share with the other members of the group.
— To teach what is involved in true leadership.
— To show how much he really loved them.
— To make them feel humbled.
— To demonstrate what true Christian community will involve for each member.
— To help them grasp the meaning of servanthood.

2. CHRISTIAN SERVANTHOOD TODAY

(60 minutes)

Individually complete the following, then, after completing the "Action Response", each person in turn shares his answers and explains why. Go around the group sharing answers to "In your Church"; then when all have shared move on to sharing responses to "In your own Lifestyle".

IN YOUR CHURCH. In what way is servanthood demonstrated in your local church? List persons and activities which model this.

How would your local church be different if it followed completely (or at least more closely) Christ's example of care and concern? What aspects of the programme would be needed to be changed?

IN YOUR OWN LIFESTYLE. Who needs me to "wash their feet"?

Write the persons' names and be as specific as you can in indicating what it would involve.

ACTION RESPONSE (10-15 min.) Write a brief letter to the person whose name you listed above.

or write a personal covenant indicating your intent to do something about what you have written (you may care to share this with the group or one other, and ask for their prayer support in carrying it out)

or write a prayer response to this experience.

CREATIVE RESPONSE (20 min.). Working as a group or in pairs, design a crest or shield to represent the kind of Christian Community which should eventuate from Christ's example of servanthood. Design suitable symbols and use colours which symbolise feelings and other aspects you wish to convey.

Additional Scripture Resources

Philippians 2:1-8
Mark 10:35-45

Acceptance and rejection

PURPOSE: To provide experiences to help participants gain some understanding of the deep feelings associated with acceptance and rejection which hopefully will lead to a greater sensitivity to and caring concern for others.

TIME: 1½ to 2 hours.

MATERIALS NEEDED: Chartpaper, glue, brush, masking tape and a newspaper or magazine for each sub-group of two.

THE PARABLE OF THE PRODIGAL SON

(40 minutes)

Read the parable found in Luke 15:11-32 from a modern paraphrase (with young people *God is for Real, Man*) using either — a good reader or — the play-reading method with three characters and a narrator (all passages quoting the three main characters are read by individual readers, the rest of the passage is taken by the narrator). Be sure to practise beforehand.

Brainstorm Session. The leader records on a chart-board or chart, feed-in based on the two following questions. Make two separate lists headed by "Father" and "Elder Brother". (In a brainstorm session no discussion is allowed during the feed-in.)
— What word describes the father's attitude to the younger son?
— What word describes the elder son's attitude to the younger son?

Generally the words "acceptance" and "rejection" appear in the lists, otherwise introduce them as summarising or including most of the words in the lists.

Bible Role Play.
Follow the outline of this method applied to this parable, found on page 108.

LIFE EXPERIENCES OF ACCEPTANCE AND REJECTION

(30 to 40 minutes)

Divide into groups of 6 or 8.
Allow spontaneous sharing on the basis of the following questions. The leader should introduce the questions one at a time allowing five to ten minutes for sharing on each question.
— When did you feel rejected by someone?
— When did someone go out of their way to make you feel included, accepted?
— When did you deliberately reject someone?
— When did you make a real effort to make someone feel accepted or included?

A FUN EXPERIENCE OF ACCEPTANCE AND REJECTION

(10 minutes)

Without giving the impression that this is an important aspect of the learning experience involve the whole group in playing Musical Numbers. Introduce it by saying the group should have an opportunity to relax after such an intensive session.

Musical Numbers is played as follows:

The players march around in single file while music is being played. Then, when it abruptly breaks off, the play leader calls out some number — and the players try to form into groups of that number. Those who cannot get into such groups fall out of the game. The music restarts; the march is taken up afresh; a new number is called — and so the game goes on until the winning players remain.

When groups form **they should clasp hands.** The leader should always choose such numbers to call as will ensure that just one or two have to drop out each time.

At the end of the game, in a jovial manner, announce that no one seemed to have any real learnings from the previous part of the session, for Musical Numbers involves a high degree of rejection for it to function!

Replay the game with everyone playing only an acceptance or inclusion role — being more concerned about others being included in the groups than themselves. Generally the game collapses in a lighthearted manner.

CREATIVE RESPONSE

(30 minutes)

In sub-groups of two make a montage of what was learnt about Acceptance and Rejection and seek to show the action each pair plan to take as a result of this session. (A montage is an art form in which pictures, headings, scraps of articles, or single words, all related to the theme, are selected from newspapers or magazines, cut out, arranged, and pasted on to a piece of chart paper.)

Conclude by each pair fixing their chart to the wall, or laying it on the floor in the centre of the room. The whole group move around in pairs discussing each chart.

PRAYER RESPONSE

(3 minutes)

Form the whole group into a large circle, holding hands if they wish, and spend a brief time in spontaneous spoken prayers or sing a hymn or chorus which is in the form of a suitable response to the session.

The Divine Enabler

PURPOSE: To enable an appreciation of the divine resources that are available through the Holy Spirit to produce the quality of group life and ministry which is characteristic of a vital Christian cell.

COMMENTS: The celebration at the conclusion of this session works best if a number of small groups have been involved. However, don't avoid it if there is only one group — consider presenting it at a large gathering, e.g. a church service.

TIME: 1½ to 2 hours.

MATERIALS NEEDED: A candle for each person, matches, candle holder (or saucer) for central candle.
For the celebration you will need white newsprint, coloured felt tip pens, craypas, paints, brushes, glue, coloured sheets of paper, magazines, hymn books.

PREPARATION: Place an unlit candle in the centre of the group on a candle holder. Give each person a candle.

THE SYMBOL OF A FLAME

(20 minutes)

— Turn out the lights and sit in the silence with eyes open for a minute or two. Try to get in touch with the darkness, think what it means — loneliness, fear, uncertainty, danger, etc.

— The leader lights the candle in the centre of the group. Each in turn lights their candle from the central candle.

— Discuss the symbolism of a flame:

— What are some things these flames are doing now?
— What are some things they have the potential to do?

(The leader may list these on a chart which has a large flame drawn at the top.)

— By the candle light read in unison, or each taking a verse in turn, Acts 1:1-14, 2:1-21 (or Acts 1:6-8; 2:1-4).

— What did the flames at Pentecost symbolise — to what extent were they a promise of things to come?

THE MINISTRY OF GOD, THE HOLY SPIRIT

(30 to 40 minutes)

— **Individually** read through Romans chapter 8 and Ephesians Chapter 4 noting on a separate sheet of paper:

— What do these passages teach us about the work of the Holy Spirit?
— Which of these points is a new thought to you?
— Which is something you feel moved to claim for your own life? What specific situation does it apply to?
— In what ways would our group be different if we let the Holy Spirit minister to us in this manner?

Small Group Work: Each share their findings. The feed-in from the first question can be listed on a chart.

PLAN A CELEBRATION

(30 to 40 minutes)

— Let the group working as a team plan something creative based on the learning experience in this session.

Some suggestions to consider:

i) Make a wall mural on newsprint using any of the materials supplied. (Coloured paper, glue, paints, coloured felt-tip pens, cuttings from magazines).

ii) Plan and practise a short play (or role play).

iii) Write the words of a song which the group sings to a well-known song or hymn.

iv) Work out a way of expressing things learned through creative movement.

v) Plan and make a series of cartoons or caricatures to form a comic strip.
Each "frame" is done on a large sheet of newsprint, then all are linked together.

Let's celebrate!

Where a number of small groups have been involved all the groups sit around the hall while each group makes their presentation in the middle of the hall or at one end.

Murals, cartoons and other artwork are then fixed to the walls.

The session could end with a few people responding in brief prayers and the singing of "We are one in the Spirit", "A New Commandment" or similar suitable songs or hymns from the "Holy Spirit" sections of traditional or modern hymn books.

Acknowledgements:

All rights to this series are claimed by the author and publishers. A great deal of material in the small group movement is becoming common domain; ideas have originated in one place and have been varied, changed, or used as a basis in others. We are indebted to such work. A small amount of material in this series has been adapted or copied from roneoed sheets, received from a variety of sources and on which there was no indication of copyright.

We are indebted too for the inspiration of a number of pioneers and leaders in the small group movement and to those who have shared new insights and thinking on fellowship, prayer and Bible study with the Church today. We have acknowledged all sources on which we have drawn, either in the text or in a list of references at the end of a chapter. We acknowledge in particular the work of William F. Barclay, Dietrich Bonhoeffer, John L. Casteel, Lyman Coleman, Gordon Cosby, Robert M. Cox, Robert C. Leslie, Sara Little, Thomas Merton, Keith Miller, Lesslie Newbiggin, Elizabeth O'Connor, Lawrence Richards, Roslyn Rinker, Charlie Shedd, Samuel M. Shoemaker, Ross Snyder, Helmut Thielicke, Walter Wink and Stephen Winward. We acknowledge too the insights shared by participants in the small group training courses and workshops.

We acknowledge with thanks the Joint Board of Christian Education, Australia and New Zealand for permission to quote from Teaching and Christian Faith Today by D. S. Hubery and from their Youth Manual; The Bible Reading Fellowship, London, for permission to quote from *Introducing the Bible* by William F. Barclay; Abingdon Press, Nashville, Tenn., for permission to quote from *A Handbook for Know Your Bible Study Groups* by Charles M. Laymon, (C) 1959; Zondervan, Grand Rapids, Mich., for permission to quote from *A New Face for the Church* by Lawrence O. Richards; Augsburg Publishing House, Minneapolis, Minn., for permission to quote from *Find Yourself in the Bible* by Karl A. Olsson, copyright 1974; Collins Publishers, for permission to quote from *A Plain Man Looks at the Lord's Prayer* by William Barclay; Harper and Row, Publishers, Inc., New York, for permission to use and abridge excerpts from *With the Holy Spirit and With Fire* by Samuel M. Shoemaker, to Ross Snyder for permission to use the outline of his Bible Study Method.

John Mallison took the photographs; our thanks to the subjects.

Front Cover Design and art work by Pilgrim International, Sydney.